ABOUT THE P

Parkbench Publications welcomes manuscripts from all aspiring authors and new writers who find their literary ambitions thwarted by other publishing companies that simply take the easy option and sponsor the 'works' of celebrity non-writers. If you have a project that is no more than 200 pages in length, submitted preferably by disc in PDF format, then Parkbench Publications will afford your proposed book the attention and respect that it deserves.

ABOUT THE FRONT COVER

For the benefit of those readers who are sufficiently interested (which ought to be everybody), the black and white chequered pattern was chosen in deference to the logo of Two-Tone Records, whose stable of artists – The Specials, The Selecter, The Beat, and Madness made my teenage 'bedroom years' bearable. Of course, the alternative would have been a photograph of the author, but the reader has been mercifully spared this after I visited a photographer and instructed her to take a few snaps of my good side. Regrettably, she could not locate it.

OTHER PUBLISHED TITLES BY THE AUTHOR INCLUDE

Harold Potty And The Goblet Of Gobbledygook
Barry Potter And The Same Old Formula
Larry Potter And The Hogwash From Hogwarts
Harvey Potter And The Temple Of Doom
Pol Pot: An Appreciation
The Life And Loves Of Pope John Paul I
A Tribute To Heinrich Himmler
The Strange Death Of The Labour Party
Tony Blair And The Last Crusade
Bedtime Stories For Insomniacs
Two Gentlemen Of Venice
John The Baptist: The Wilderness Years
The Merchant Of Verona
Oliver Twisted
Bleak Bungalow
KJ Rolling: My Life At The Top, Volumes 1 to 37
Jose Mourinho: The Humility Years, 1984 to 1986
David Cameron: The Nazareth Years

Any of the above titles can almost certainly be obtained by sending a cheque for 15 thousand Euros to: Parkbench Publications, 22 Downing Street, London, SW1. Hurry while stocks last. Special offer: Buy any one of the above titles, and receive a free copy of the greatest-ever work of fiction – The Labour Party 1997 General Election Manifesto.

WHAT THE CRITICS SAID

I have already submitted samples of this outstanding publication (sic) to a handful of publishers, and I have just received my first rejection. I have been informed that my project is, and I quote, "a very interesting proposal, which will undoubtedly prove popular when published." Since my rejection is couched in such sweet, prophetic terms, I will not name and shame Elena of JBP, which I have lovingly abbreviated. Anyhow, here are some of the comments that I have received from those truly blessed with a sneak preview of my magnum opus:

> "Sehr gut und wunderbar. It is almost as readable as Adolf Hitler's 'Mein Kampf'" – Heinrich Goring, Fuhrer of the Bavarian Cricket Umpires' Association
>
> "... a mesmerising masterpiece from a literary genius who is clearly destined to become a huge star of stage and screen for many decades to come." – Professor Paul Hislop, editor of Pseudo-Intellectual Weekly
>
> "This book is dangerously addictive. I couldn't possibly recommend it to any of my clients." – Iggy Reed of The British Cocaine Suppliers' Society
>
> "This bible of virtue is second only to the Koran in its holiness." – Ayatollah Thingymajig of Teheran
>
> "... a giant amongst literary works, perhaps only surpassed by Noel Edmonds's book." – Sister Pauline Brown, co-editor of Nuns Quarterly
>
> "It would of been good if it had not been written by such a ****ing ****." – Vinnie Wise, chairman of the Home Counties' Football Hooligans' Club

“Brutal, honest, and brutally honest, this book will stand the test of time as a monument of twenty-first century culture.” – John Chapman, book reviewer for Flying Pickets Monthly

“A hundred times more hilarious than any awful BBC middle-class sitcom, aliens and robots will have endless conversations on their mobile telephones in centuries to come about the merits of this publication.” – Walter Strachan, assistant editor of the Strathclyde Cat Burglars’ Gazette

“... contemptible, lamentable, outrageously pathetic rubbish that no self-respecting, bandwagon-jumping, spineless publisher or literary agent should ever consider entertaining.” – David Skinner, acting chairman of the Association of Bandwagon-Jumping British Literary Agents And Book Publishers

“I’m not sure about the contents of this book, but the cover is a work of art, surpassed only perhaps by Michelangelo’s inclusion of cabaret, jellies, and kangaroos in The Penultimate Supper.” – Leonardo ‘di Caprio’ Da Vinci, art critic

“What kind of a title is that for a book? Why don’t you get yourself a proper job, like everybody else?” – me Mum

HOW TO COMMIT SUICIDE IN TEN EASY STEPS

K.J. Rolling

PARKBENCH PUBLICATIONS

Published in Great Britain by Parkbench Publications,
PO Box 1081, Belfast BT1 9EP

A CIP catalogue record for this title is available from the
British Library

ISBN 978-0-9555756-0-0

Designed and typeset by Bookcraft Ltd,
Stroud, Gloucestershire
Printed and bound in Great Britain by
CPI Antony Rowe, Eastbourne

In the name of God
and the defenders of
Derry, I declare this
book open for the
transaction of business.

ACKNOWLEDGMENTS AND HALL OF SHAME

This masterpiece (sic) was originally conceived as the autobiography of a hugely talented non-celebrity but like Frankenstein's monster, this beast of a book has taken on a life of its own in which the author has offered his tuppence worth on a whole galaxy of topics. If you wish to reply to this thought-provoking, outspoken, opinionated outsider, then feel free to let off steam of your own to my e-mail address of: kjrolling@hotmail.co.uk

In the meantime, I would like to thank the following who made this book possible: the psychiatric nursing staff at Rampton, the Samaritans who have patiently listened to me for many interminable hours, and also to the two policemen who climbed up on to the top of the high-rise flats, and persuaded me after four and a half hours to come away from the edge. A big thank you to Mummy for giving birth to me, and to my multitude of family, friends, apostles, disciples, crazy fans, followers, hangers-on, and sycophants who have collectively suffered me for far longer than anybody could deserve. I owe also a deep debt of gratitude to my proof-reader, Rio Ferdinand, as well as to Paris Hilton and Robert Mugabe, who both suggested amendments to my text when I submitted a draft of it for their scrutiny. Merci beaucoup to my publishers, Parkbench Publications, for believing in my project, and in the hall of shame lurks the following spineless publishers who were both too precious to entertain this earth-shatteringly, ground-breaking work of art and lacking in entrepreneurial spirit to invest in an unknown quantity, namely: Appletree, Belfast; Aurum Press; Blackstaff, Belfast; Carlton Group; Lloyd Publishers; and Michael O'Mara Books. There were others who declined to accept my masterpiece but at least they shall remain unnamed and unashamed because they had the good grace to reject me quickly, rather than jerk me around for several weeks, like the previously listed.

This book is dedicated to any wonderful reader who agrees with everything that I write, laughs in all the right places, and who then proclaims to various friends and family that K.J. Rolling is an adorable, easy-going genius, with a flair for comedy, as well as flares for comedy. More particularly, this book is dedicated to anybody who is so spell-bound by my magic that they go and buy another copy, as well as to those who use my book to prop up the sofa and then buy another copy for the mother-in-law.

INTRODUCTION
I JUST WASN'T MADE FOR THESE TIMES

Have you ever felt like speaking your mind or getting a few things off your chest, but maybe you resisted the urge for fear of upsetting the neighbours or your family and friends? Well, the author, who prefers to be called K.J. Rolling, has decided that he cannot hold it all in any longer, and so he has lovingly chosen to unleash a whole host of ramblings and rants that reflect his own growing sense of alienation. Consequently, the writer has decided to offload thoughts and words which are not for people who are easily offended, but which may cater for those who are easily amused.

Why take this provocative and drastic step? Well, the author has had a tendency to amuse people with his anger and to anger people with his humour, so it is only right and proper that this non-celebrity should provide equal portions of angry and humorous observations of life in the twenty-first century to keep any brave reader occupied. Whilst avoiding the Tony Soprano route of burdening his thoughts on a therapist, the author has generously opted to share his outspokenness with all those wonderful people out there in book-reading land.

This publication is akin to Adolf Hitler's last will and testament, in which a plethora of denunciations are made of various people and organisations. However, it is not all negativity. There is hope within too. The author hopes that you will pick this book up from the bookshop shelf, hopes that you will buy numerous copies, and hopes that some souls will agree or at least laugh at the sentiments contained within ... hopefully. Oh, and the author sincerely hopes that if you read this book in bed at night that you remember to switch off your bed table lamp afterwards and that you don't have nightmares from reading this seminal document.

The author has chosen anonymity, taking his cue from John and Yoko's 'bagism' project in which the controversial couple elected to conceal themselves in a bag so that their genuine calls for world peace would not be distracted by attention on their appearance. Similarly, the writer wants all and sundry in your thousands to focus on the words and 'listen without prejudice' (to coin a phrase from that great philosopher George Michael) and not concern yourselves with who he is.

One note of warning needs to be included. This publication contains strong language. Words such as 'heavy', 'muscular', and 'powerful' may appear occasionally. My solicitor has also cautioned me to emphasise that all characters in this book are entirely fictitious, especially the celebrity ones, so don't bore me with threats of libel and don't tickle me with accusations of defamation of character. Some of you 'entirely fictitious' stars are so far down in the gutter that you don't have a character left to de-fame. If you are starting to sweat and tremble at the pages that lie waiting ahead in ambush, then go and run back to your nearest bookshop and exchange this publication for Russell Bland's life story. I won't hold it against you. Oh by the way, be solemnly warned that the copyright details are not to be infringed, so if I find any future publication containing such words as 'the', 'and', 'to', 'from', and 'of', I will know that you have stolen them from my book without my prior permission. To any such writer: a plague on your house.

If you still feel equipped to persevere, then don't just sit there. What are you waiting for? Get reading, and discover where those Iraqi weapons of mass destruction are really hidden.

THE OLD TESTAMENT

GENESIS

In the beginning, God created man and, to cut a long story short, I was born (under a wand'rin star) many many years ago in a maternity hospital far away (while shepherds watched their flocks by night), because there was no room at the inn.

I was the product of what sociologists might describe as a 'mixed marriage': my mother was a woman, and my father was a man, so I had a very difficult upbringing. In fact, my family were so impoverished that we were the only household in our housing estate who didn't own a gun. My parents, bless their cotton socks and pink pyjamas, always wanted me to go far – preferably as far as possible. The furthest however that I could manage was Parkhurst on the Isle of Wight. I would have went further, but I couldn't get over the wall.

Sorry Mum and Dad, but I was a fucking accident – literally. I was the product of a night of pre-marriage passion that had more consequences than the loving couple had anticipated. Yes folks, I wasn't exactly planned. It was an inglorious debut for me, and I have striven hard to maintain my habit of ensuring that things don't go according to plan ever since. Mind you, when you plan anything involving humans, then you are almost certainly doomed to failure.

My long-suffering parents were thus obliged to marry a little sooner than might otherwise have been the case, and to be fair to them, their marriage proved durable, and I cannot complain about parental abuse or neglect, which leads to the obvious question of what has prompted me to become an alienated, angry young(?) man? The answer is circumstances, pure and simple... or put another way –

people! I am increasingly coming round to the opinion that the world would be a happier, more peaceful planet if there were no people on it. Retreating further from the well-intentioned but mindless morons who violate my lebensraum, I feel that I no longer belong in this world where my peers get their thrills from copious amounts of liquor and from watching violent movies at the cinema.

Most annoying of all, I am surrounded by self-important types in their big cars, big houses, dressed in their shirt and tie, who have not got a fraction of my numerous talents. The sentiments of 'The Philosopher' in the Old Testament book of Ecclesiastes that, inter alia, 'life is useless' are readily endorsed by this writer. Before you drool over my miscellany of ramblings, rants, and really ridiculous 'rubbish' which form the very epicentre of my alienation, let us first embark on our Magical Mystery Tour , so come with me into a land where the eyes of man have never set foot.

MY FAMILY AND OTHER ANIMALS

My late father, Joseph, whom I had previously worked for, was a carpenter. My mother, Mary, is as pure as the driven snow.

Oh alright, calm yourselves down. The true Lord did prophesy that many would come along and say that I am the Messiah. Okay, I will retreat from this apparent blasphemy before I get stoned. Mind you, Bobby Dylan did once suggest in 'Rainy Day Women Numbers 12 & 35' that everybody has to get stoned. To quote Barney Gumbel (my role model) from *The Simpsons*, "Jesus will be turning in his grave". Right, that's enough. Please Lord, forgive me. You know that I am just mischievous and naughty.

My earthly family are a fairly unremarkable, humble, and publicity-shy lot, so I will spare them the unauthorised use of their names. There is a saying that you can choose your friends, but not your family. Well, I honestly would not swap my family for anybody. More to the point, I doubt whether any sane person in either hemisphere would swap places with my parents. After all, being a parent of mine is a lousy job and poorly paid too.

I even like all the members of my extended family circle. The trouble is that I am growing less inclined to go near any of my relatives. An occasional visit to an aunt and uncle or cousins only results in a torturous session of being badgered with a whole host of probing questions. This rigorous cross-examination is designed to ascertain how much progress (if any) that I am making, and to draw comparisons with their offspring. Personally, I am tired of the mentality of measuring one's worth in terms of how many houses I own, or how big my car is, or where I go on holiday. If life is indeed a race, then it is where you finish that counts ... and just for the record I am in the pits ... getting my tyres changed. I even remember making a rare appearance at a barbecue where a bloke asked me if I owned my house or paid rent for it. Why ask that? If I only pay rent instead of a mortgage, does that render me a lesser human being? You stupid, materialistic, disapproving fools.

I am reminded of *The Simpsons*' episode where it was feared that the next-door neighbour Ned Flanders had murdered his wife, Maud. Then she appears, to inform the startled Simpsons that her absence was due to her attending a Christian course where she was learning to be judgmental! I suspect that there are a few members of my family circle (and plenty more besides) who have completed such a course. Many members of my family circle will be a little surprised, even shocked by my publication, but it has been liberating for me to break down the door of keeping my thoughts hidden and fulfilling my parents' desire that I should be seen and not heard. Well folks, my dear friend Michael encouraged me to be real, although maybe I am just a bit too real for many people. Anyhow, excuse me, while I go and take my pills.

CRACK COCAINE

Nine out of ten cat owners said they preferred it ... to heroin.

SMALLTOWN BOY

My home town is a fairly unremarkable locality, possessing some areas that are nicer than others, some shops that are better than others, and some people that are nicer than others. Like many small towns, it is merely a haven of small town and neighbourhood gossip. It actually reached the stage where I could not bear to be out walking along the footpath without imagining a passing motorist pointing out to his or her passenger: "there goes whichyoumacallit, y'know, the son of whichyoumacallit, who lives next door to whichyoumacallit, and who used to work for whichyoumacallit." In small towns, you cannot break wind without everybody knowing about it – not that my wind-breaking antics are particularly newsworthy. What sums up my home town are the lyrics from Morrissey which suggest that the rain falls down on a humdrum town that has dragged me down.

ANOTHER BRICK IN THE WALL

"When I was at school, education could go hang, so long as a boy could hit a six, sing the school song very loud, and take a hot crumpet from behind without blubbing" (extract from *Blackadder Goes Forth*).

When I was a little nipper, Norn Iron had the two-tier, antiquated education system in which eleven year olds were shunted, usually without their consent, into either grammar schools for cleverdicks or secondary schools for 'thickos', depending on their performance at the eleven-plus selection tests. Only at the behest of one-time education supremo, Martin McGuinness no less, is this system being earmarked to follow its English cousin to the knacker's yard to be replaced by something vaguely related to comprehensive schools.

It was quite amusing watching the stink that MrMcGuinness created as 'his' reform stirred the otherwise dormant Northern Irish middle-classes to an activity alien to them – protest. Yes folks, while the working classes of both communities tore each other's hair out and plenty more besides, during 'the Troubles', the I'm Alright Jack Nimbys of the Northern Irish middle-class sat idly by, tut-tutting the sectarian bloodbath. It took a threat to their own self-interest to arouse the blue rinse bourgeoisie from their conservatories.

Norn Iron, you see, has been 'blessed' by an education system where the intelligent Davids and Sarahs at eleven go on to highly-reputable academies of learning to be taught to become captains of industry, while the stupid Jimmys and Sharons at the same tender age brace themselves for schools notorious for producing, perhaps through no fault of their own, many under-achievers. A welter of education statistics has confirmed the disparity in achievement between the high-flying grammar schools and the considerably less academically successful secondary schools. The absolute need to take my pew at a decent seat of learning was therefore seen as a life-changing crossroads moment in which I simply had to fulfil my early promise at primary school, during probably the best years of my life, and ensure success at the 11-plus.

So it came to pass that this young infant prodigy with 'brains to burn' (although I have yet to fulfil my potential and incinerate them, despite a couple of flirtations with hallucinogenics) managed to pass the Eleven-plus. I seemed destined for academic success and a wonderful career, going to work each day armed with a briefcase, shirt and tie (oh yes and trousers too) to do my stint at the office, throwing my weight around and then driving home in my big car to my big expensive, suburban house. Somehow, this high-flier has successfully managed to avoid realising this pseudo-American dream which has permeated many burghers on our side of the big pond.

Where did this young smart Alec go so horribly wrong – or even right? Well, I was actually encouraged by my father to consider a possible venture into the crazy world of an architect. Fortunately, this young man had other ideas. I mean, have you ever seen the sketch from Monty Python's Flying Circus about the accountant, Mr Anchovy, who visits the vocational guidance counsellor whereupon the accountant (might as well be an architect or office worker or whatever paper shuffler) confesses to the career adviser his desire to become a lion-tamer? The counsellor (played by John Cleese) helpfully suggests that the accountant (played by Michael Palin) should not attempt to get to the position of lion-tamer in one drastic career re-shuffle, but instead via stages, starting peculiarly with banking. Quite how banking is a step away from accountancy towards lion-taming is open to question, but this young genius at least managed to swerve these dreadfully dull but eminently respectable white-collar positions – much to my parents' disappointment.

Personally, I blame my school for my development/deterioration, but then who doesn't? You see, my academic factory is one of those Norn Iron pompous grammar schools that takes itself too seriously. This pseudo-public school is more interested in winning the apparently coveted rugby union Schools' Cup to achieve bragging rights than in the academic progress of its students which is taken for granted, given that many of the pupils' mummies and daddies are teachers and dare I say it, accountants and bankers. Whether any of them progressed towards the exalted position of lion-tamer, I am blissfully unaware.

Oh yes, I excelled at O Levels and A Levels, earning a passport to university, a truly pioneering step for someone from my family circle. The nearest any of my relatives got to university was driving past a local campus. Despite my academic 'success', I felt like a second-class citizen at a school where it was my misfortune not to be a rugger bugger. I had a very good attendance record at school and there was no bullying or disciplinary issues of note. I was just an anonymity at secondary school, an apprentice loner, largely keeping my large head down in apparent practice for the system that lay ahead. Mind you, although never 'picked on', I did still float from one clique to another, without belonging in any particular circle – a trait that I have long since perfected. I don't have any particularly fond memories of attending an all-boys school. Like George Mallory, the Everest explorer, I simply climbed the mountain of school because it was there.

I was especially interested in such 'useless' subjects as history and politics, but a remedial no-hoper at the sciences. In fact, I was a spectacular failure at physics, which was like a foreign language to me. In the school Christmas exam, I earned the flattering mark of 17 per cent which was airbrushed up to 20% in my school report, on account of a school policy that dictated that minimum marks of 20% had to be recorded on one's report. My 'folks' were horrified at the disgraceful 20%. Little did they know that the powers that be had generously improved my marks. I managed to fluke my way to a staggeringly impressive 28% in the summer physics exam, whereupon physics and I went our separate ways, very much by mutual consent. Had it not been for the multiple-choice format of the physics tests, I honestly would not have merited a double-figure percentage score. Some of my guesses in those physics tests must have been spectacularly wrong – as well as occasionally right. It calls to mind a Punt and Dennis sketch entitled 'Science Is Fun', I think, apparently in which they explained how helpful it was to have multiple-choice questions which usually included an absolutely absurd option that obviously should be ruled out immediately. For example, four possible answers for one question could be: is it a) an electron; b) a proton; c) an atom; or d) Geoff Hurst in the 1966 World Cup Final. Tragically, I think that too many of my 'inspired guesses' in the physics exams were of the Geoff Hurst variety – much to the consternation of my physics 'master'. I never used the term 'master', as this young rebel without a cause never quite saw anything masterful about individuals who are regarded as 'men amongst boys, but boys amongst men'. My physics under-achievement robbed me of a high-flying career as a rocket scientist, devising even more weapons of mass destruction for Iraq. NASA has never quite recovered from the near-mortal blow of my physics tragedies.

What I find most objectionable about Norn Iron grammar schools in particular, as I stand on my soapbox, is that they produce arrogant, sarcastic know-it-alls, perhaps like me, who are not taught enough humility and respect for everybody. Oh yes, schools try hard to juggle several balls in the air at once, I acknowledge this, but what on God's earth is the point of learning about ancient Greece and trigonometry formulae whilst many life skills are neglected? For me, it is fundamentally important that teenagers are taught such basics as knowledge of cars, home insurance, life assurance, mortgages, drug and alcohol awareness, even self-defence, not to mention how to cook and even change a light bulb. Too many eighteen-year-olds, like yours truly, once upon a time, go out into the big bad world, snowed under with qualifications and high expectations, thinking that they know it all about everything, when in reality, the poor dears know nothing about anything. Maybe if I'm fighting for my life on a hospital bed or even attempting to raise a family, expertise in ancient Greece and trigonometry formulae will suddenly become belatedly useful, though I doubt it.

WELCOME TO MY WORLD

Do you despair of the foul-mouthed, attention-seeking teenagers and twenty-somethings in our society? Are you dismayed by the talent-less stars and celebrities who infest our magazines, newspapers, and television screens? Are you demoralised by the greed of fat cats and self-important sporting and musical 'heroes'? Are you angry about how taxpayers' money is wasted by careless politicians who think that 'fact-finding' all expenses paid missions to places in the sun are more crucial than health service waiting lists? Are you losing the will to live, weighed down by the injustice in your life? Then, welcome to my world. Make yourselves at home, pull up a chair, while I go and stick the kettle on.

FIRST IMPRESSIONS

So, what do you think of the show so far, folks? Are you going to storm back to the bookshop and angrily demand a refund? I hope that you held on to your receipt. Well, you ought to. Do you think that I am bad, mad, or just plain sad? Well, I am not too bothered what your reaction is. I am just grateful that you were courageous enough to buy a copy of my book. Oh, and my mortgage lender is thankful too. May God bless you and all that sail on you.

Actually, I believe that first impressions are frequently misleading. One should never judge any book by the cover. As for people, well, how often have we discovered that the pleasant person with the smiley face was not all that they were cracked up to be, while the person whom we initially had reservations about, turned out to be someone surprisingly good. Perhaps we cannot see the wood for the trees (a recurring theme), or maybe we foolishly allow our initial opinions of other people to be formed on the basis of their accent, appearance, clothes, hair, or skin colour. Anyhow, let us re-adjourn to the proceedings.

LIFE IS A PERPETUAL SHOWER

Like most semi-normal people, I get up in the morning, have a shower, go outside, and get soaked going to work in a shower. I get to work. My colleagues are an absolute shower (and some of them need a shower). When I go out for lunch, I am in another shower. When work is finished, I go home in yet another shower, and on reaching home I settle down to watch the shower that masquerades as entertainment on television. I then go out in a shower and join the shower at the local pub where I shower myself with booze, before returning home in another shower. I then finish the day by having another shower.

Interested in more expensive car and home insurance,
then let
MOORE THAN
quote you unhappy from the works of Shakespeare,
including "a horse, a horse; My kingdom for a horse."

BIG PEOPLE AND SMALL PEOPLE

Top military strategist and Chief of the Imperial General Staff for much of the Second World War, Lord Alanbrooke, wrote in his outspoken diaries scathingly of one or two colleagues, such as Field Marshal Alexander, and one or two exalted politicians, whom he described as 'small' people. It got me thinking that indeed there are a lot of individuals in our society who may not be tall in stature, but are 'big' people, while there are many more people who may be six foot or more in height, but who are essentially 'small' people.

Let me explain. Northern Ireland, where I grew up (to a debatable extent) is full of small people. They consist mainly of big men who all choose to follow Liverpool or Manchester United because their mates do the same. They join a band or orange lodge because their mates do the same. They go boozing at the week-end because, guess what, their mates do the same. A sense of individuality and independent-thinking has been sucked out of many such people. Many young men (and women) surrender their own sense of self-awareness to go with the flow and follow the crowd. People are petrified to dress differently or have attitudes contrary to their peer group. Do not be fooled, folks. Big men with tattoos, muscles, t-shirt, and jeans are frequently small people who are so insecure that they hide themselves in a group of so-called mates. They would cheerfully bring their mates along to their job interview or if they were having a bath. Just ask someone what they did at the week-end, and you will receive the predictable response that "me and my mates did..." and "me and my mates went..." Yes 'small' man, but what did you do?!

Hats off to the big men and women who can stand on their own two feet, who don't have to cling desperately to fellow co-dependents, and who are not afraid of their own company. Furthermore, they don't deliberately tailor their allegiances, clothes, and values to fit in with so-called accepted norms. To the big men and women who may not be tall in stature, who do not feel that they have to surround themselves with so-called friends, I salute you.

P.I.G.S

Winston Churchill once remarked that cats look down at us, dogs look up to us, and pigs treat us as equals. Pigs, as we all know, are obese, gluttonous, and filthy. There are a lot of human creatures who could be equally described in such terms. I concede that it is all too easy to make generalisations, but hey, we are all guilty of it. Therefore, when I have a swipe at the binge-drinking, tabloid reading, soap watching members of our beloved society, I am referring to the pig-like behaviour of P.I.G.S, or people in general. Of course there are many wonderful people who have integrity, humility, and perform acts of kindness, thoughtfulness, and selflessness. My beef is with PIGS (people in general) who are loud, attention seekers, who lack intelligence, don't listen to reason, and who throw numerous stones from within their glasshouses. Why are city centre pubs (especially at the week-end) over-populated with herds of these PIGS? People in general (PIGS) fill me with dismay, but bravo to the good, sensitive, thoughtful people in this world. They know who they are.

TEXTING

God forgive me, but I despise people who are constantly texting, instead of talking. Texting was invented for teenagers and people who cannot spell. By the time that you have reached 22 (and almost come of age) you should be growing out of texting and short trousers. Instead of which, I am surrounded by chavs who want to communicate in code to one another. Worst of all are the insecure types: "my boyfriend hasn't spoken to me in fifteen minutes. I'd better send him a text." Get yourselves a life!

ERIC IDLE:LUST FOR GLORY
An epic starring Mel Gibson, with animation from Walt Disney.

THE LONELY CROWD

Am I alone (probably) in being absolutely disgusted by the filthy language of people around me in the workplace and in the streets and bars? Nobody seems able to use words such as 'please' and 'thank you'. It costs nothing to be polite, folks. Instead of which, countless mindless morons experience little trouble in including 'fuck' and exclaiming 'Jesus Christ' in virtually every horrible sentence that they produce. How do such godless wonders end up with so many 'friends'? I definitely do not belong in a world with such creatures whose only idols are a bottle of vodka or beer, which they pay homage to every week-end. Far too many silly young people think that it is sexy to drink half a bottle of vodka. Sorry children, but here is a little secret that I will reveal to you all: there is nothing remotely attractive about someone with half a bottle of vodka in them. Is there anything more ugly in fact? Well, if I'm sad, what does that make them?

It is both contemptible and lamentable to find most students and twenty-somethings who attempt to obscure their insecurities and self-loathing by herding together at week-ends to numb their senses with large doses of alcohol. Oh yes, we can put it down to 'part of growing up' or 'just a phase that we all go through', but there is something terribly lacking in individuals who sacrifice large chunks of their spare time in the pathetic pursuit of getting drunk. If certain folk could only see themselves when they are intoxicated or visit a few hospital wards to witness the consequences of alcohol abuse, they would realise that there is nothing remotely sexy, cool, or glamorous about over-indulgence in alcohol consumption.

In Belfast for example, you are nobody unless you are seen to be raising a glass with your mates in a club or wine bar at the week-end. Many poor souls like to surround themselves with so-called mates so that they can forget who they are and what they are, and invest precious time and money into so-called socialising. How often have you witnessed such 'sociable' people end up bickering, bitching, snarling, and fighting both amongst themselves and with anyone who dares to look at them the wrong way. So much for being sociable. Frequently, a group of dreadfully insecure mates go out, they cling to one another for dear life, they don't befriend anyone else, and nobody is welcome to penetrate their sad little circle. There is scarcely a sadder sight in the world than scores of young people, some in their teens, queuing impatiently at a bar, desperate for a quick fix of poison. These people must truly hate themselves.

WASTED LIFE

When I was nine years old, I used to beat up other children at primary school.
Well, it seemed like a good idea at the time.
When I was twelve years of age, I started to go absent from secondary school.
Well, it seemed like a good idea at the time.
When I was fifteen, I began sniffing glue and smoking twenty cigarettes a day.
Well, it seemed like a good idea at the time.
When I was eighteen, I started drinking heavily and smoking dope.
Well, it seemed like a good idea at the time.
When I was 21, I graduated on to heroin.
Well, it seemed like a good idea at the time.
When I was 24, I knocked down and killed a child while under the influence of alcohol.
Well, it seemed like a good idea at the time.
When I was 27, I tried to hang myself in my prison cell.
Well, it seemed like a good idea at the time.

Lies, malicious gossip, sensationalism, and trivia.
Only in *THE SCUM*. Priced 30p at any newsagent.

ACTION FILMS

Is it my imagination or do most cinema-goers get terribly bored if someone hasn't been killed or violently attacked within the first five minutes of a movie? Precious few people, and they are precious, seem to care much for plot or dialogue. Action films cater for sad, impressionable chavs who draw inspiration from the on-screen Neanderthal nonsense, and replicate the behaviour in their own pathetic lives. Is it no coincidence that thugs like violent movies and own dangerous dogs? You can learn a lot by the 'taste' or lack of it that many people possess in films. Any bloke who likes Green Street or any Guy Ritchie/Vinnie Jones rubbish is someone I would not want to associate with. The trouble is that many silly little girls are just so inclined to cling on desperately to hard-drinking, hard-living, Billy Hard. It is a recipe for blood, toil, tears, and sweat. When will you people learn?

Movie billboards such as Miami Vice which portray the cops wearing dark glasses, and Mr and Mrs Smith, featuring the deliciously sexy couple of Angelina Jolie and Brad Pitt lend such films a glamour and gloss they scarcely deserve. Anyone who thinks that such movies are cool and sexy should pay a visit to a few hospital wards to witness the glamorous consequences of violence. Lying in a bed with your body all mashed up is far from cool or sexy. Action films ultimately cater for the brain dead who are easily amused, in other words for people with a single figure I.Q.

BANDWAGON-JUMPING

The great British media and public love nothing more than to indulge in their favourite pastime of jumping on a bandwagon. Let us observe the cases of George Best and John Lennon, two cultural icons. These individuals were the recipients of much scorn and tut-tutting during their lives, on account of their behaviour and lifestyle. Yet when they die, they suddenly have airports named after them and have lavish praise heaped on them by a plethora of bandwagon-jumpers. I sincerely hope that when I am finally pushing up the daisies, that those individuals who have frowned upon me and unleashed various abuse and disapproval when I was alive are at least consistent when I am deceased. To jump on any bandwagon and pay posthumous tributes to me would almost certainly prompt me to turn in my grave. Please don't feel the urge to name an airport after me, although if you must, you can name a park bench after me. In fact, I promise to return and spookily haunt anyone who dares to start any chorus of 'he was a wonderful human being'.

FUNERALS

A lot of people seize the opportunity of a funeral to take a day off work, put on their Sunday best, and then pay a moving tribute to the deceased, whom they hadn't seen or spoken to for many months or years even. When I cease to be, becoming an ex-parrot, bereft of life, joining the choir invisible, I sincerely hope that a multitude of distant relatives and even more long-lost friends don't come out of the woodwork, lay down their tools and overalls, and proceed to lavish praise on me. If they really want to pay their respects to me, my 'countless' legion of friends and relatives should maintain their attitude of apathy and indifference, as perfected during my existence. Let me rest in peace. Mind you, I do have a tendency to wake up once or twice in the middle of the night, so when I am 'sleeping' in my grave, I suspect that I will awaken every few years.

MY OBITUARY

Family and several friends were shocked, though not entirely surprised, to learn of the sudden death of K.J. Rolling, the supremely talented author, genius, and misfit, after a brave but futile battle against alienation and loneliness.

A handful of people jumped at the opportunity to take a day off work and pay their insincere, clichéd respects at the funeral service which passed without incident apart from when the deceased opened the coffin lid and grumpily exhorted the vicar to keep the noise down, before returning to sleep. At the graveside, one relative was heard to remark: " I will miss his sarcasm", while another mourner added: "I do not know how I will cope without his cynicism". Rolling's local pub landlord was visibly upset (at the thought that his takings would never be the same again) while a representative from the dead man's mortgage lenders also expressed his regret at the sudden loss of life after a lengthy illness. It was however some consolation to the assembled few that the deceased passed away noisily in his sleep.

The vicar (and part-time actor) spoke movingly of how the former author had been the very essence of warmth, pleasantness, and sheer joy, adding that no party was complete without K.J. Rolling sulking in the corner or letting off steam about something or other. The mourners were assured that the deceased would be joining Adolf Hitler, Saddam Hussein, Genghis Khan, and Joe Stalin in heaven.

At the conclusion of the burial, some relatives retired to a nearby hostelry where they drank several toasts to the deceased and recalled with considerable mirth, K.J. Rolling's various embarrassing exploits, a session which predictably lasted into the wee small hours, before bracing themselves for the reading of the will to ascertain who would be the unfortunate recipient of his record collection and clothes.

Perhaps the most fitting epitaph for K.J. Rolling was conceived by himself: a hugely under-rated actor, comedian, dancer, politician, singer, and writer, there was nothing wrong with him that a little love and understanding wouldn't have cured.

VOTE SINN FEIN

Support the administration of British law and order in Northern Ireland, and VOTE SINN FEIN.
Support the Police Service of Northern Ireland, and VOTE SINN FEIN.

DEATH: A GOOD CAREER MOVE

If, like me, you are going nowhere slowly, money's too tight to mention, or you are in a dead-end job, or you failed to catch the buses to love, happiness, prosperity, and success, perhaps death would be a good career move. It has certainly worked wonders for the formerly flagging fortunes of Kurt Cobain, Jimi Hendrix, John Lennon, Marilyn Monroe, Jim Morrison, and Elvis Presley, to name but a few individuals who have managed to successfully revive and/or maintain their careers without breathing a single breath. In fact, just consider the lyrics of 'Suicide Isn't Painless' by Carter The Unstoppable Sex Machine, and you will see the folly of suicide unless you are a struggling 'star'.

STOP YOUR SOBBING

If you are complaining about your job, spare a thought for those who cannot get one. If you are moaning about the lengthy building repairs to your house, spare a thought for those who are homeless. If you are moaning about only being able to go abroad once every year, spare a thought for those who can scarcely afford to put food on their tables. If your children are giving you a hard time, spare a thought for those couples who cannot produce offspring. If your loved one is upsetting you, spare a thought for those souls who have nobody to love them. If your bout of influenza is making you feel miserable, spare a thought for those people who are terminally ill. There are an awful lot of drama queens out there who need to dry their tears and count their blessings. As Ray Davies once suggested, there are a lot of people who need to stop their sobbing.

AGONY AUNT

Good cover versions are hard to find, but among my favourites are The Byrds' interpretation of Bob Dylan's 'My Back Pages', and also The

Jimi Hendrix Experience's re-working of Mr Zimmerman's 'All Along The Watchtower' is awesome, while UB40's cover of Jimmy Cliff's 'Many Rivers To Cross' deserves special mention. Another cover version which I have a particular liking for is Grace Jones's version of The Pretenders' 'Private Life'. I really 'dig' Chrissie Hynde's lyrics, which Jones, ably assisted by ace Jamaican duo of Sly and Robbie, does tremendous justice to.

Oh yes, when I hear from anyone that "my girlfriend and I are going through a bad patch" or "my boyfriend has walked out on me", I just want to quote the lyrics Of 'Private Life'. Pouring your heart out to me about your relationship problems is like going for a lovely walk and then returning to tell a cripple that your poor legs are hurting. Unless your loved one is terminally ill or your children are starving, then don't give me your drama queen routine. If after visiting a children's leukaemia ward, you still feel that you have a hard luck story to share, then you are very welcome. Otherwise, dry your tears and save your breath before you bore me to death with your sex life complications.

EVERTON FOOTBALL TEAM'S ONE HUNDRED BEST-EVER THROW-INS
(including the twelve-yard one against Northampton in a 1973 pre-season friendly)

ANGER

There are a lot of angry people about – even angrier than me. Are they not getting much sex either? There is something horrible about certain individuals who take great pleasure in raising their voice, playing the role of a drama queen and making some unfortunate wretch look small. I also find that too many people are very horny in their cars, wanting to beep furiously over nothing in particular. If I had a pound for every storm in a teacup which is blown out of proportion, I could take an early retirement. I must concur with the abuse dished out by the late Graham Chapman in Monty Python's 'Argument Clinic': To all you angry, frustrated little people "shut your festering gob, you tit, your type makes me puke".

Highlights from the GLASGOW RANGERS 2006–2007 SEASON (Length: 5 minutes)

DRIVE MY CAR

We all have our 'moments' whilst driving. My own grievances focus largely on the apparent reluctance, even refusal, of many 'responsible adults' to use their indicators whilst driving. Is it just ignorance or another bad-mannered manifestation of the 'don't give a stuff' mentality that plagues our roads, footpaths, homes, and workplaces? To get to the point, this young man remains baffled why many drivers wish to keep their movements in their vehicle concealed from other road-users. Do you ignorant people think that I am a mind-reader? Indicate which exit at the round-about that you are planning to take, if you would be so kind. Adding more insults to more injuries, and yes I am feeling increasingly wounded, many individuals not only don't indicate when they should, but horror of horrors, indicate when they don't need to! Why, if the lane that you are in goes right only, are you indicating to go right? Even more ludicrous are the desperados who break the world land speed record when rushing through amber lights. Do these silly people expect the subsequent red light to stay red for an hour and a half? Those cretins who just have to overtake all and sundry are not driving their wife, who has gone into labour, to hospital. No, they are in a frantic hurry to be home in time for Coronation Street. Gosh, they lead such important lives. Oh, who will rid me of these turbulent motorists?

RUSH HOUR

There is no quality of life in sitting miserably behind the wheel of a car for what seems like an eternity, as traffic crawls along at what is ironically referred to as 'rush hour'. My suggestion for Belfast and a few other British urban centres is that more businesses need to take the initiative (which is what business firms ought to specialise in) and start their employees at earlier times in the morning. If we had more people starting at the staggered times of 6, 7, and 8 in the morning, there would be much less motorists all heading in the same direction between 8 and 9am each weekday. Consider the advantage of working from 7am to 3pm. Children could be 'collected' from school', instead of killing time around shopping centres each late afternoon. There would also be an opportunity for a little shopping, which is denied anyone on the 9 to 5, Monday to Friday treadmill. I accept that this solution is far too crazy and/or sensible, but ultimately maybe several companies could be given a financial incentive to start earlier each morning, thus alleviating traffic congestion during the laughably-titled 'rush hour'.

LONDON BUSES

A lot of people are frustrated by the tendency for London buses to be absent for fifteen minutes or more and then at least two appear at once. I, moreover, am perplexed by the enormous amount of London buses that are all travelling to a mysterious destination, entitled 'Not In Service'. Could anyone in Greater London kindly inform me where this location Not In Service is? I must protest in the strongest terms at the large volume of buses all apparently going to this Not In Service area, which is clearly under-populated, because there is never any passengers on this route. I would humbly suggest that London United runs fewer buses to the Not In Service locality, because the route isn't very popular, and concentrate on providing more buses to more populated areas. I would also like to draw attention to the bus passengers in London and elsewhere who choose to sit in the 'aisle seat' and not occupy the window seat so that nobody can sit next to them. They even feel that their bags of shopping are entitled to a seat whilst others on the bus have to stand. To all those ignorant men and women who feel that their bus ticket provides them with not one but two seats, shame on you.

BLACK PEOPLE

I must confess that I am opposed to any further immigration to London. There are far too many people moving to the capital from Belfast, Dublin, Glasgow, Manchester, Newcastle, Prague, and Warsaw. They come to London, steal 'our' jobs, claim benefits, and before you know it, they will be opening their own corner shops. It must stop immediately. No seriously, I do admit to having previously been apprehensive of the flood (according to the British press) of Commonwealth immigration that has 'swamped' Britain over the last five decades. However, on reflection, I must congratulate the successive Conservative and Labour governments for their open door policy. If it had not been for the foresight of many politicians in past years, Britain would end up with about two medals in the Olympics – one for cycling, and one for rowing. Black power, I say.

My biggest concern for black people in inner city Britain is that their biggest enemy is not the British National Party but the young, armed gangsters who are ruining their neighbourhood. A lot of liberals and politically correct lefties need to wake up to the fact that black people are more at threat from their own youngsters than from white supremacists. Black youths have killed far more black people in the last few decades than any fascist racist ever has.

Have you ever wondered why black men are so much better at sprinting? I think that I have discovered the answer. Young black men spend their teenage years being chased by the police, so that by the time that they reach their twenties, they are experts at sprinting. It must be fun being a black person in Britain. I mean at night, when you walk along the pavement and you see one or two black youths approaching from the opposite direction, you think 'well, I think I'll cross the road and take no chances'. It must be amusing for black people to see all these terrified whites criss-crossing the road at night.

I once went for a job interview in a Brixton reggae shop. The proprietor asked me if I was a racist. I said yes I am. Before I could say another word, the ex-Jamaican threw me out. If he had let me finish my sentence, he would have discovered that I cannot stand white people.

BRITISH MUSLIMS

Being a semi-brave soul, or perhaps a fool with a death wish, I shall dare to speak on the controversial subject of Muslims in Britain. What fascinates me is that a lot of Muslims leave Asia and the Middle East for a better life in Britain, where they have expectations of a home, a job or state benefits in the absence of employment, as well as all the legal protection and human rights that are apportioned to any British citizen. However, a point that needs to be addressed to all immigrants, particularly Muslims, is that Britain has expectations of its new residents. Britain expects its new members to obey all areas of the law, and among other things, new citizens are expected to raise their children in the education system in much the same way as everyone else is required.

However, what we find increasingly is that many people come to Britain and ghettoise themselves, and form de facto independent states within specific areas of various British urban localities. This 'ourselves alone' separatism manifests itself in such ways as Muslims wishing to have separate education in which their offspring are perhaps taught values and attitudes which are at a tangent from what non-Muslims accept or expect. Yes, I am all for individuality and not necessarily mind-numbing conformity. However, fears are being raised that the extreme fascist followers of Islam would gladly introduce sharia law to parts of Britain. What is worse is when the Islamic extremists, egged on by their liberal, politically correct solicitors, complain that Britain is a police state. It would be outrageous if it weren't so ridiculous. Someone needs to remind the Muslim separatists that if they have misgivings about the administration of law and order and justice in infidel Britain, they can always take their chances in the arab states, north Africa, not to mention certain Muslim-dominated states of the Middle East and Pakistan where their collective record on human rights leaves even more to be desired than the imperfect administration of justice in the 'police state' of Britain.

This must not be perceived in the well-worn, tiresome terms of a rabid racist. Indeed, it is most regrettable that anybody who expresses concerns or even constructive criticism about the Muslim community is immediately scorned as a white supremacist. The tragedy is that until Britain's Muslims take a full role in contributing to their new country without divorcing themselves whenever it suits them, the far right in the British National Party will reap the benefits of increasing anxieties about the mentality and behaviour of British Muslims. Britain's Muslims must learn to be more tolerant of dissent, which is part and parcel of life in a free speech society. Our new citizens must be willing to listen to non-Muslims' anxieties, and seek to address them. Wouldn't it be good if British Muslims were prepared to enlist in our armed forces and police service? Continuing failure to do so only arouses the suspicion that British Muslims do not approve of our country's rule of law and our foreign policy. This then begs the question of how can people 'settle' in a country where they are at loggerheads with that country's requirements?

I would like to finish by paraphrasing the late John F.Kennedy by stating that British immigrants, most notably Muslims, should not ask what their country can do for them, but what they can do for their country. A continuing failure to address this question only serves to increase alienation and racial tension, which racists, of which I am emphatically not one, will take advantage of.

The contents of this page have been reluctantly removed so as not to cause offence to the highly-sensitive, super-touchy Islamic fundamentalists.

HOUSE-SHARING

Sharing a house with other people is perhaps second only to raising children as the hardest task in the world. It is difficult enough to live with one's family and loved ones, so how much more taxing is it to share a house with complete strangers? House-sharing is almost a rite of passage for all students nowadays. Perhaps the only consolation with sharing a home with strangers is how 'educational' it is to survive in the company of people from different walks of life, with their assorted attitudes and values.

I recently shared a humble abode in London, where a man moved in, who told me that he had been living in the Belmarsh area of east London for the previous eight years. Shortly after, a young woman moved in to our house. She apparently had been living in the Holloway area of north London for the previous six months. Not long afterwards, a gentleman who had spent the last twenty years residing in the Broadmoor area also moved in. Well, all I can say is that I don't know what these areas are like or what kind of upbringing these individuals have had, but ever since they moved in, a lot of items have gone missing in the house.

SHELTERED LIVES

The latest Aussie soap. Join the suburban residents of Celibacy Street, Sunsetsville, and catch up on the latest developments. Next week's episodes include Victoria Spoiltbrat's dilemma over which shoes to buy, while Mr and Mrs Temporarily-Married are throwing a dinner party for their rich business friends. Meanwhile, Lucy, pining for her boyfriend, falls in love for the twelfth time in the last six months – this time with Rick, the dashing young property investor. Starring: Danii Minogue, Rolf Harris, Elle Macpherson, Barry Humphries, and Shane Warne.

THE RISE AND FALL OF A PROPERTY TYCOON

If you are ever feeling sorry for yourself, then get in touch with me and soon you will realise how truly wonderful your life really is. For example, consider the following sad tale. I once had aspirations of owning a large portfolio of houses and/or apartments. Putting my money foolishly where my mouth is, I took the plunge into property investment, having been enticed by several property investment schemes which promised the earth.

The trouble was that I invested in low value houses in inferior areas which regrettably though quite predictably attracted inferior tenants. My heart was all but broken by tenants and property management firms who seized the opportunity to run rings around a wet-behind-the-ears absentee landlord. One particular source of frustration is when tenants make protracted claims for housing benefit, as I have learnt to my literal cost. One woman lived in a house of mine for virtually six months and left without paying a penny, and before her housing benefit application had been approved or rejected. Consequently, the local council in Doncaster refused to back-date housing benefit to a tenant who no longer resided at my house. I was obliged to take this lady to a small claims court where it was decreed that she should pay the outrageous sum of £5 per week to settle her debt of approximately £1,500 to me. It will take her about six years to re-pay the money she owed for six months' rent. It would be funny, if it wasn't so tragic. I had another family at the same address who were served an eviction order for non-payment of rent. The police were required to remove them, but not before the fearless junkie swine had moved back in again. I have lost count of the number of times that I had to hire a locksmith to tend to my crumbling property empire. Oh by the way, if there is anyone out there who knows the whereabouts of Mr Greg Madison, formerly of Blind Lane, Darlington, but possibly now residing in the Costa del Crime, I would be ever so grateful.

I eventually decided that it would be prudent, or at least less hassle, to sell my castles. The exercise, though a profitable one, was my 'Dunkirk' – an evacuation, but empires are not preserved by evacuation. Anyhow, my brief and bitter foray into the world of business was perhaps more of a valuable education than any worthless school lesson. All that remains for me to say is that if you ever need useful advice on how not to invest your life savings, make me your first port of call!

NEW FOOTBALL PHONE-IN
Call The Samaritans between 5pm and 8pm each Saturday, if your football team makes you sad and suicidal.
Telephone 0845 909090

YOU COULDN'T MAKE IT UP

Once upon a time, this handsome young prince paid a visit to a university travel agents in September 1992 in order to book a flight to stay with Mummy and Daddy that subsequent Christmas. So far, so good. The problem was that when this young gentleman presented himself at the check-in desk at Manchester Airport three months later, he was informed that his ticket reservation had been cancelled (or more likely, wiped by a computer error) approximately sixty seconds after it had been issued. To make a bad situation rather worse, I was also informed that the flight in question was completely full, which left the airline (I think that it was British Airways) in a bit of a quandary.

However, help was at hand, as the dashing pilot generously allowed me to trespass the cockpit for the duration of the flight by occupying what is called the 'jump seat', which is effectively a seat that folds out from behind the cockpit door. Perhaps the only other alternative would have been for me to masquerade as a member of the cabin crew, but mercifully, the passengers were spared my performance as a trolley dolly. What therefore promised to be an unholy mix-up culminated in me being a temporary co-pilot, enjoying the spectacle of the aeroplane landing on the runway with a 'ringside seat'. Perhaps every cloud does indeed have a silver lining.

IT'S TOUGH AT THE TOP

Once upon a time, this semi-handsome prince shared a flat in south-west London with Tim-Nice-But-Dim. Tim decided to go on a month's vacation to Thailand but mischievously informed his silly Filipino co-dependent girlfriend that he was required to make a month-long, work-related trip to Germany. I was expected to be acquiescent in Timmy's naughty act of treachery. However, I did not approve of his deception and to cut a long story short, Tim adjudged me to be surplus to requirements when he returned to his flat, after his adventures in the Far East. Timmy and I had a clash of personalities. He has none and I have several.

I then 'squatted' in the semi-squalor surroundings of a flat in west London which I shared with its owner, a sexual deviant Liberal Democrat parliamentary candidate, who shall remain nameless because he still harbours faint hopes of taking a seat at Westminster to make Mummy and Daddy proud of him. Subsequent to this, I acted as a babysitter for a house of mine in County Durham whilst its sale was being completed. Then, lo and behold, one fine sunny spring day, whilst the birds were singing in the trees and the sun was shining – though not necessarily on me – the sales transaction was completed, and a black gentleman duly arrived at my former house to inform me that I should leave his house. Defying all racial stereotyping, there were no fisticuffs and this gentleman even gave me a lift to Gateshead where I planned to board a train and return to my Liberal Democrat buddy's humble abode in London.

The trouble was that later that evening when my 'friend' returned to his flat and found me to his horror firmly ensconced once again in his living room, he told me that I had outstayed my welcome. Having violated his lebensraum, I had to pack my bags, though thankfully not for 'resettlement in the east'. For the first time in my life, I found myself homeless. I spent a few nights at bus shelters and making repeat journeys on London buses to kill time and stay remotely warm. It was peculiar to say the least, walking the streets in the company of the people of the night. One woman joined me at a bus stop and asked for a cigarette which I could not give her. She then proceeded to lift discarded cigarettes from the pavement. I then spent several nights in a rented car before a cousin lovingly granted me permission to irritate him and his flat-mate for several days.

There isn't necessarily a happy ending or moral to this story, but I think that I can confidently stake a claim to being one of a select group of 'personae non grata' to be evicted from two houses in the space of ten hours. I don't know ultimately if I am more sinned against than sinning, though I fear the latter is more valid.

WOMANISING

Men are so predictable – it's true. When a guy spots the girl of his dreams, he usually makes hard work of attempting to befriend her. Mind you, most women are hard work. What almost always happens is that Romeo at the critical juncture of his existence when he approaches Juliet for that first fateful time suddenly gets an attack of itchy scalp as he starts nervously scratching at his head whilst uttering the immortal words: "I was wondering if..." Any young woman who hears "I was wondering if ...." being expressed by a head-scratching nervous wreck has a fair inkling of what is going to follow. Many ladies immediately respond with the instinctive reply of: "I'm washing my hair." I once was so tongue-tied that I blurted out: "I was wondering if you would be washing your hair tomorrow night", to which I was informed, "no, I'm washing my hair." Mind you, would you go out with a tongue-tied, frantically head-scratching personage? No, I wouldn't think so. It's worse even in a noisy night-club where you find yourself shouting loudly at a member of the opposite sex: "do you want a drink?" Would you feel thirsty in such a moment? No, I wouldn't think so.

What baffles me about young women nowadays is that they are so contradictory and two-faced in their attitude towards dating. Frequently, many women want to conform to gender stereotyping and keep their purse padlocked and their hands firmly in their pockets for the duration of an entire date, leaving the male to pay for the cinema and/or dinner and/or drinks and/or coffee and/or a taxi. I would estimate that of the fourteen women that I have dated in one form or another over the last two and a half years, at least a dozen of them were richer than me, and the reason that they are richer than me is that they don't dip into their pockets! Perhaps, I have 'soft touch' written on my forehead. Personally I don't have a major problem with this scenario, provided that the woman is making an effort in other ways. However, what I sometimes find is that lo and behold, some young women suddenly don't want to conform to gender stereotyping by dressing up attractively and wearing make-up. I suspect that there are too many young middle-class women who, as a legacy of feminism and dressing down and wearing drab outfits as students, wish to carry this bolshie dress sense into later life. I was always taught that one should dress to impress, a lesson that I have put into practice with varying degrees of success. It is all very well young women stating that they don't want to be regarded as ornaments or trophies, but if I, yes me, make more effort in preparing for a date than the female, well it ain't saying much for her. The way some young women dress so casually for a date makes me wish that I had just pulled on a cardigan and tracksuit bottoms. The bottom line is that most of us are average-looking individuals, and therefore we need to dress up and make an effort in order to look better. Only supermodels and supremely handsome guys can wear pyjamas and Wellington boots and still look good. It might be perceived as a case of the pot calling the kettle black, but I suspect that there is a very good reason why there are so many single women in their thirties and beyond. By making the effort to look good and dare I say it, smell good, we are telling the other person that the occasion is important and that they are worthy of respect. To do less invites a casual attitude and creates nothing but anti-climax.

Meanwhile, more and more desperate Dans and Dianes are exploring the alternative avenue of internet dating. The trouble is that too many women (and men) simply want to hide behind their computer screens in their comfort zone and cultivate a farcical e-mail relationship, thereby virtually dating a virtual boyfriend in a virtual relationship. Mind you, it spares some of them the immense hassle of dressing up and wearing make-up. What a drag that would be. Worse still, there are many internet 'lovers' who are not what they seem. This fool has bitter experience of internet fraudsters who exploit the internet to scam strangers. Just take a look through anti-scam.org to view the remarkable world of internet scams.

Speed-dating is becoming an increasingly popular form of 'mating'. Maybe originally it was regarded as a vehicle for desperate types, but it is a dynamic means of meeting and talking to a wide range of approximately twenty members of the opposite sex. One of the advantages of its format is that a whole host of women have to suffer you for three or four minutes, when otherwise they might wisely choose not to. What I have discovered from attending such events is that many guys appallingly tick every lady in the hope of getting several dates. Where is the sense in that? Most women on the other hand wisely tick only a handful of guys, although there are some women who think that they are so precious that they cannot even give the benefit of the doubt to one or two men. I find that one's success at such an event is at the mercy of the slings and arrows of outrageous fortune. Due to the dynamic of such an occasion, each man follows the same guy in front of him to the next table for his next date. If the guy ahead of you looks like Worzel Gummidge and is half-drunk, then your chances of making a good impression behind his trail of destruction are quite considerable. If alternatively, one is immediately behind Mr.Suave, then one is snookered. Furthermore, it gets pretty exhausting talking in quick succession to about twenty people, so one's frame of mind is more positive after one or two dates have been safely negotiated, yet one starts to tire after about fifteen 'dates'. Therefore, one is more inclined to be favourably disposed to someone that they meet early on, which is unfortunate as the last person that they speak with could be the nicest, most attractive person at the event. There is also the benefit that individuals are informed after the event who liked and didn't like them, so it tends to be less embarrassing than your usual rejection scenario. At least, it is an improvement on the tragic but regrettably all-too-familiar situation painted in The Smiths' single, 'How Soon Is Now?'

SPEED-DATING

I once went to a speed-dating event. Well, okay, I have been to numerous speed-dating ventures. However, one night in particular is recalled. I was handed at the outset a list of the names of the female 'competitors'. A few of them, I noticed, had what I considered strange Christian names – in fact more than a few. I remember a couple of Esthers, amongst others. It wasn't until about my fifth 'date' that my other half helpfully pointed out to this slow learner that this was a Jewish speed-dating event. She advised me to demand my money back, but I assured her that I was not too bothered – being as I am not an Islamic fundamentalist. Another Jewess later suggested that I should ask for a refund, but imagine the scene if I started angrily protesting like a 'bigoted' anti-Semite that I did not want to be participating in a Jewish speed-dating event. No wonder the Christian names were 'odd'.

This tragic story has been a fitting metaphor for my action-packed 'love life'. However, I will not bore you this time with the sad tale. There simply aren't enough tissue boxes in the universe to cope with your tears of sorrow and tears of laughter at my romantic liaisons. Suffice to say that the only time that I have women chasing me is when I owe them money.

LEFT TO MY OWN DEVICES

Even Jimi Hendrix complained of loneliness in the excellent 'Burning Of The Midnight Lamp'. Yes, 'sex-God' celebrities can seem terribly lonely. In fact, a roll-call of some of the most lonely people on the planet would reveal such surprise names as Kurt Cobain, Brian Jones, Jim Morrison, and Elvis Presley. Contrary to popular myth (and I am familiar with a few myths) there is nothing wrong with being a loner. There is a lot to be said for having your own space, being master of your own castle, and coming and going as you please, without answering to anybody. In fact, if many over-heard pub conversations are to be believed, there are a lot of 'happily married' men who would cheerfully swap their ball and chain life sentence for an irresponsible 'lost weekend' of bachelor living.

If only it was that simple. I admit that I suffer from a superiority complex. I truly believe that there are few people worthy of my company. No, I'm not a pompous ass, honest. It is just that the older that we become, the more selective we become about what activities we choose to do and especially choosy about the company we keep. I simply feel that there are few men whose company I can suffer, unless they are devotees of Enya, Mozart, or Jamaican ska. To tell the truth, most men are predictable bores, as suggested in my piece on 'big people and small people'. I grow tired of the same routine, foul-mouthed conversations about cars, fights, and imaginary female conquests. Most men, it is my considered opinion, simply talk a good game, or to coin a phrase are all mouth and no trousers. When I venture into a public house to watch a football match on the box, I cheerfully steer clear of the noisy blokes who clearly either don't get out much or who cannot handle their liquor. I have far too much self-esteem to associate myself with the lonely crowd. There are frankly few men that I admire or respect.

I am not afraid to admit that it is the company of an attractive, well-groomed, humorous, intelligent, caring and loving woman that I seek – nothing more, nothing less. It is indeed one of the great conundrums of modern world history that I find myself fast approaching forty years of age and still 'senza una donna'. Surely Miss Right must be out there somewhere. Where are you, my dear? Come to me. I am impatiently waiting for you.

I am not an oil painting, but I truly believe that I am a good man who deserves so much better. I think that it is my turn to do regular stuff and catch the bus to love and happiness. Regrettably, I live in a society where one is depicted as an oddity if one is not married by thirty years of age. However, bad things do happen to good people. It is simply an injustice that I have not located my perfect match and soul mate. Instead of which I seem to be a magnet for loonies and plain Janes. Less deserving types have been able to take for granted something that I have to jump through hoops and work exceptionally hard to attain. I actually empathise with people who are wrongly executed such as Derek Bentley or imprisoned for crimes that they did not commit such as the Birmingham Six. I await my liberation from my unjust spell of solitude. It is my turn. My time has surely come. Who is brave enough and beautiful enough to step forward and rescue me from myself?

I'M STILL WAITING

It is so frustrating that us impatient souls spend large chunks of our lives waiting ... for something or other. Why is it that we seem to have a lengthy wait for a refund or cheque in the post, but bills and final demands arrive in a flash? I actually don't have much sympathy anymore for all you 'waiters' out there. It is just 'terrible' that you have to wait in a supermarket queue for five minutes. It is simply 'intolerable' that you have to wait at a red light for two minutes. It is frankly 'outrageous' that you have to wait a full three minutes at the bar for your fourteenth pint of lager. It is 'criminal' that you have to wait for ten minutes in the queue at the departure gate before embarking on your two week holiday in the sun. Oh you poor people have got it so tough.

Well, I have had to wait not twenty minutes, nor twenty hours, not even twenty weeks, nor even twenty months, but twenty long years to find someone special to give me the love that yes I deserve, so excuse me if I don't give a stuff about your 'lengthy wait' dramas. I sense that my family and friends think that I should just 'settle' for anyone remotely interested in me (perhaps like they did?). I don't think so, folks. Just imagine if you have had to wait, horror of horrors, for an hour and a half at a restaurant to be served your first course. How would you then feel if the waiter brings you, not a delicious bowl of soup, but a plain cream cracker. Well, ladies and gentlemen, I have waited so long that I expect someone really 'tasty', and definitely not a plain cream cracker.

I COULD HAVE BEEN A CONTENDER

In my humble opinion, there is a thin dividing line between success and failure. I consider myself on the wrong side of this line. However, to all you fellow losers out there, be encouraged that circumstances can improve very quickly. You are perhaps just one successful job application and/or chance encounter with a stranger from changing your life for the better. Despair can be transformed to fulfilment in seemingly no time. I believe it is possible. It is what keeps me going and persuades me to get out of bed each morning.

If we take a look at the world of sport, it is abundantly clear that tiny margins can separate glory from humiliation. For example, a batsman in cricket can be dropped early in his innings before he has scored many runs, only to survive and hit a double century. A simple dropped catch can be the difference between embarrassment and triumph. In football meanwhile, a striker can be dropped for the next match after failing to score in his most recent game. However, he may have produced good saves from the goal-keeper and hit the woodwork once or twice. These defining moments can determine someone's career. Also, a failure to win, arising out of a match where his team miss a penalty and have one or two goals disallowed can lead to the sacking of a manager. In horse racing, a horse can win a race unexpectedly when the runaway leader falls at the last fence. It has been known to happen!

I feel that I have hit the post and crossbar once too often. It is my turn for a little glory or fulfilment. In my negative moments, I am losing the will to live, but enough of me still thinks that the good life is out there somewhere.

I WILL GO TO MY GRAVE

I have obtained 10 O Levels, 3 A Levels, two degrees; written books, appeared on television and radio, and in newspapers; worked in a wide range of jobs in a variety of locations, and bought and sold several houses. However, if circumstances don't improve (and fast), I will go to my grave, believing that I am a loser who deserved a lot better. I don't belong in a world where I am misunderstood and under-valued. An old man once confessed to me that he was glad that he was going out of this world, and not coming into it. Life as I know it and have perhaps wasted it holds no value for me any more. I look forward to virtually nothing. Stop the world; I'm getting off. Occasionally, to borrow the sentiments of that nice cheerful Morrissey, I lie in bed, thinking about life and death, not sure about which is more appealing.

MISTLETOE AND WINE

There is something absurd about the exchanging of gifts at Christmas time. If I buy someone a present, he or she feels obliged to reciprocate, which only serves to cheapen my generosity. Therefore, the giving and receiving of gifts is merely a glorified business transaction. What is equally ludicrous is the following scenario: Person A gives Person B £50 for Christmas, and a few days later Person B gives Person A £20 for Christmas. Would it not have been less hassle if Person A had just given Person B £30 for Christmas? Then we have the situation where Person A gives Person B a £20 Boots voucher as a present, and then Person B gives Person A a £20 Boots voucher also. The only real winners here are Boots – and shops in general. I have nothing against Boots, honest. It's just that when I wandered around one of their stores one day, a shop assistant helpfully asked me if I required assistance, and when I stated that I could not locate any Wellington's anywhere, I was horrified to learn that Boots don't actually stock boots. I have struggled to recover ever since from this trauma. Anyhow, we have all been horribly hoodwinked into the tiresome practice of showering gifts on the people in our lives to prove that we love them. What staggering nonsense. Being there for your loved ones in moments of crisis is how you express your love. Ritual token gestures are neither here nor there. They are just designed to keep card shops in business. When you rely on a card to tell someone that you love them, there is clearly something lacking in your relationship.

I now spare myself that dreadful Oscar-winning performance each Christmas morning whereupon one opens Christmas presents and expresses unbounded delight at some unwanted gift. "Thank you so much for those orange socks. I have always wanted a pair since I was about five years of age." "Wow, a brown cardigan. I can't believe it. I was about to buy one of these in the January sales." Rumour has it that Chambers of Commerce and various retail organisations organise their own carol services where they pay homage to the Three Wise Men. Where after all would the wonderful 'advent' season be without the 'advent' of the three kings from the east? Can you imagine them carrying their precious gifts over many miles nowadays? They would probably have to travel to Bethlehem in a Securicor van for fear of getting mugged. Alternatively, if they really wanted to be wise, it might be less hassle to each present a Boots voucher.

Ultimately, Christmas is just an orgy of food and alcohol consumption, in which office parties try to outdo each other in terms of excess and bad behaviour that would have made the Vikings blush. I know of one work dinner dance that resulted in one or two stabbings and a female fist fight. Ah yes, it almost always ends in tears. People invest so much energy and expense into Christmas that they slide into a post-Christmas, New Year depression. How pitiful. Thank God that He sent his only begotten

Son along to save the world and be born in the atrocious conditions of a cattle barn. Had He not done so, we would all have to find some other excuse to embarrass ourselves with too much alcohol each December – not that many of you heroes of the wine bottle ever need an excuse.

WHAT'S ANOTHER YEAR?

Why do so many 'follow the crowd', silly 'small' people celebrate the New Year? They like to delude themselves that their lives will magically improve with the advent of a New Year. What poor fools. Unless people are prepared to change their existence for the better, they should forget about celebrating another likely twelve months of under-achievement and unfulfilled expectations. If people are really serious about transforming their lives, then why wait until January the 1st? I guess that New Year's Eve, like Saint Patrick's Day, is just one of those days when a multitude of bandwagon-jumpers have to drink themselves stupid. Gosh, what a glorious start to any new year. It speaks volumes for someone's commitment to new resolutions when he or she spends the first four hours of the new year drinking themselves sick, and the next twelve hours sleeping it all off. Is that what you call turning over a new leaf?! Ultimately, the only thing worth raising a glass to on December 31st is the fact that the passing year will not be inscribed on your tombstone.

As for this eternal loner, a new year represents more opportunities to suffer embarrassment, failures, humiliation, rejection, and setbacks. One resolution that I will practise is a refusal to ask anyone out. Being friendly doesn't come naturally to me. As a matter of fact, it is bad for my image. However, on the fleeting occasions when I have plucked up the courage to befriend someone and when I then ask one or two individuals out on a 'date', they look at me in horror, as if I have suggested performing open-heart surgery on them, without using anaesthetic. How dare they. No, I resolutely won't be coming out of my shell for that scenario again. So, go on and run after the foul-mouthed, binge-drinking, tabloid-reading, tattoo-wearing morons out there. Is it any wonder then that you silly little girls need a New Year's Eve drinking session to escape from the mess that you call a life. Happy New Year? Don't make me laugh.

A YEAR IN THE LIFE OF A LOSER

January: Make and quickly break New Year's resolutions.

February: Employ a temp secretary to reply to the plethora of Valentine's cards that I have received.

March: Drink myself silly to commemorate Saint Guinness's Day.

April: Eat one too many Easter eggs to celebrate the resurrection of the Messiah.

May: Suffer the spectacle of an FA Cup final between two teams that I loathe.

June: Attend a barbecue, during which I am confronted with the following questions: "are you married?"; "do you have a girlfriend yet?"; "have you ever had a girlfriend?"; "do you prefer men?"; "do you own your own house?"; "what part of town do you live in?"; "how much rent do you pay?"; "how much money do you earn?"; "what kind of car do you drive?"; "how old is your car?".

July: Sit in traffic queues whilst 'Christian' loyalists march along the middle of the road.

August: Spend eight hours in a queue at Heathrow Airport.

September: Postpone my birthday for several years, denying that I am a year older.

October: Get stopped by a shop security guard, who accuses me of leaving the store without paying for the Hallowe'en mask. I protest that I'm not wearing one.

November: Go into hibernation, spending an increasing amount of time wrapped in a duvet.

December: Emerge temporarily from hibernation to go Christmas shopping, but sprint out of each shop whenever the next awful Christmas pop song is played. Celebrate the birth of the Saviour by drinking fifteen vodkas.

HOW TO COMMIT SUICIDE IN TEN EASY STEPS

Step 1: Get born, without your consent, being cruelly plucked from the warmth and comfort of your mother's womb.

Step 2: Be smothered with love and affection, and spoiled with sweets and toys as a brat, foolishly expecting such generosity to be replicated by everybody thereafter.

Step 3: Go to school where your sense of individuality and uniqueness is chiselled away in a desperate attempt to have you transformed into a round object to fit into a round hole.

Step 4: Succeed at school, thereby creating expectations that you cannot possibly fulfil.

Step 5: Go to university and waste three or four years studying Hegel and Kant by day and how to consume alcohol and drugs by night.

Step 6: Go to work to be bossed around by little Napoleons who possess a tiny fraction of your talents.

Step 7: Play the dating and mating game, during which you are shocked to discover that mummy and daddy's special little person is not so special to members of the opposite sex.

Step 8: Marry the first fool who expresses the remotest interest in you, and then raise nine or ten ungrateful children who demand everything and give back nothing.

Step 9: Retreat to the local pub on an increasingly regular basis, to reflect on what went wrong.

Step 10: Stick your head in the oven.

HOW DO YOU SOLVE A PROBLEM LIKE GRAHAM NORTON?

A ten-episode series set to lighten up Saturday night entertainment on BBC1

THE NEW TESTAMENT

HISTORY LESSON

Why do so many people like to escape into the fantasy world of *Star Wars, Lord Of The Rings,* James Bond, and Harry Potter, whilst neglecting the real world of history? Is it because if we were to look closely at the sadistic Romans, Vikings, Nazis, loyalist terrorists, and Irish republican terrorists, we might see ourselves in the mirror?

TRAITOR'S GATE

I am in awe of central London, especially its historical landmarks. Still towering head and shoulders into the skyline of the metropolis, above its neighbours, is the appropriately named Tower Of London. This remarkable building stands as a monument to a time when England's administration of justice would have deterred any asylum-seeker from seeking a safe haven in our soft touch country. Pride of place, or should I say infamy, belongs to the menacing Traitor's Gate, standing erect only yards away from the River Thames, waiting to 'welcome' traitors to such luxurious, five-star accommodation as the dungeons of the White Tower. Anybody who made the fateful boat journey through Traitor's Gate would not unsurprisingly have feared the worst. In the unenlightened times of Tudor England, any soul convicted of treason was perceived as an enemy of the state, the sixteenth-century equivalent of a terrorist bomber. Traitor's Gate was effectively the entrance to 'death row' and the exit to life. Few people escorted through this notorious gateway to the Tower lived to tell the tale. One such 'survivor' was the future Elizabeth I who was sent to this royal prison on the orders of her half-sister, 'Bloody Mary', who feared a Protestant insurrection in the 1550s.

London's deserved status as one of the world's greatest cities is being seriously undermined by the gun-toting young gangsters who are terrorising their communities. In my opinion, anybody who terrorises their neighbourhood is my idea of a terrorist. Perhaps the Tower Of London should come out of retirement and open its imposing gate by the river to 'warmly welcome' the young terrorists of inner-city London.

THE MYTH OF ANNE BOLEYN

Good old 'Harry of England', Henry VIII, was a fat, horrible hypocrite. Like many a noble monarch, Henry liked to sleep around, whilst demanding that his spouses be devoted to him alone. Two 'unfortunate' souls, Anne Boleyn and Catherine Howard, failed to live by the tyrant's rules, and lost their heads – literally. Catherine's crime was that she had an appetite for members of the opposite sex as many other healthy teenage girls would have.

Meanwhile, Anne Boleyn has remarkably been treated even more kindly by history. True, it was tragic that she should be cruelly taken from her infant daughter, the future Elizabeth I. However, what few people seem to realise is that Anne was public enemy number one, a conniving, manipulative, and scheming individual, whose affair with the king had wrecked his marriage to the long-suffering, but hugely popular Catherine of Aragon. There was also the small matter of incurring the wrath of the Pope with the result that the king was excommunicated, and obliged to form his own church of England. Anne Boleyn would probably have made very good tabloid fodder – such was the resentment that she aroused. Perhaps her untimely death and martyrdom was a good career move.

THE TRAGEDY OF THE FIRST WORLD WAR

Did you know that Kaiser Wilhelm II of Germany used to wear a glove on one hand and carry a glove in the other hand in a vain attempt to conceal the fact that one of his arms was considerably shorter than the other? Did you also know that the Kaiser was Queen Victoria's favourite grandson, and that he was present at her bedside when the Empress of India breathed her last in January 1901? Are you also aware that the German emperor rode at the head of the procession alongside his cousin King George V at the funeral of his disapproving uncle, King Edward VII, in 1910?

The tragedy of the First World War is that the massive carnage in the mud and trenches of both western and eastern Europe was the result of a family 'tiff' between cousins Wilhelm II, King George V, and the Russian Tsar, Nicholas III. What was even more tragic was that the likes of Adolf Hitler stepped in to the void to denounce the 'November criminals' for allegedly stabbing the undefeated army in the back. The little Austrian corporal went on to persecute Germany's Jews, many of whom had served alongside the Viennese tramp in the cause of the Kaiser. The rest is history.

THE MYTH OF THE SECOND WORLD WAR

We like to congratulate ourselves that the eventual victory of Britain (the United States and several other countries helped a bit too) prevented the absolute annihilation of European Jewry in the Second World War. However, British national governments barely registered a whimper when the Nazis started persecuting German and Austrian Jews long before the outbreak of the global conflict. Britain was even most reluctant to accept Jewish refugees fleeing Nazi terror. Yes, the

Allies belatedly liberated the death camps, but not before an approximate six million wretches had perished. However, what prompted Britain's reluctant participation in the hostilities in September 1939 was Germany's violation of Poland's sovereignty. The irony was that at the 'successful' conclusion of the bloodshed six years later, Poland was forced to surrender her independence to the equally villainous Soviet Union.

THE MYTH OF WINSTON CHURCHILL

Winston Churchill, a descendant of military genius John Churchill, the Duke of Marlborough, first made a name for himself with a daring escape from captivity during the Boer War. Perhaps torn by a desire to emulate the heroics of his famous ancestor and by a desire to sustain his political career longer than that of his father, Randolph, Winston Churchill was *un homme du destin* who seemed to be born to cope with the national emergency that violently erupted in the spring of 1940. In the previous four decades of the twentieth century, Churchill experienced fluctuating political fortunes, perhaps born out of his tendency to 'cross the floor' of the House of Commons. Starting his career as a Tory, Churchill transferred to the Liberal Party, before switching his allegiance once more to the Conservative Party. Small wonder therefore that Churchill accumulated a few political enemies along the way, so that by the time that he warned the National governments in the 1930s about the dangerous foreign policy of appeasing the dictators, Churchill was 'persona non grata' in government circles, perceived as a backbench has-been with an axe to grind. Amongst other things, Churchill had been the original hard-line Home Secretary before the First World War before becoming a below par Chancellor of the Exchequer in the latter half of the 1920s. However, it was Churchill's response to the challenge of two world wars which he is most remembered for.

Remarkably, Winston Churchill had a miserable time in the First World War after he was made the scapegoat for the failure of the naval expedition at the Dardanelles – his brainchild. Having 'flopped' as First Lord of the Admiralty, Churchill spent time serving in the trenches of the western front, before being restored to Lloyd George's coalition government in the capacity of Minister of Munitions.

By contrast, Churchill emerged like a phoenix from the ashes to galvanise Britain's lone resistance to Nazi Germany in 1940 and the first half of 1941. Having been a firm opponent of independence for India and the abdication of Edward VIII in December 1936, Churchill was a most reluctant appointment as Prime Minister. Ironically, it was the Labour Party who were more keen on his promotion than the Conservatives. Churchill's initial defiance of the enemy was all the more noteworthy when one considers that the likes of his former colleague and 'boss' David Lloyd George advised that semi-defeated Britain should sue for peace. Larger than life Churchill refused to throw in the towel, and after initial military setbacks in France, then Singapore and Tobruk, Churchill presided over a transformation in Britain's war effort, ably assisted by the emerging superpowers, the Soviet Union in the east and the United States in the west.

However, what is questionable is Churchill's status as a great wartime leader. His relations with the military were frequently strained. Churchill blamed his generals for excessive caution and he frustratingly demanded to know if Britain's army had a single general capable of winning a battle. Ironically, when Field Marshal Montgomery emerged as a military hero, his prime minister was occasionally consumed with jealousy towards someone who dared to steal the limelight from him. Britain's military leaders were also horrified by Churchill's sense of reckless adventurism. Far from being a great strategist, Churchill could never see the bigger picture, preferring instead to infuriate his military aides with his wild, half-baked proposals. The great war hero's fondness for alcohol also did nothing for the confidence of those around him. Prone to tantrums and depression, Churchill was at his best in a crisis, but once the allies started winning the war, the British prime minister was surplus to requirements. Winston Churchill would dearly liked to have fought and even die in the conflict.

He was always desperately keen to get close to enemy lines – such was his abandon, and a personal highlight for him would have been the occasion when he relieved himself in the River Rhine in March 1945.

Unlike President Roosevelt, Churchill did survive the successful conclusion of the Second World War in Europe, but was then instantly despatched from 10 Downing Street by an electorate that acknowledged his value as a wartime leader, but which questioned his potential to reconstruct Britain. Few would scarcely have imagined that six years later Churchill would be restored to power and he confounded all expectations by living until 1965, fittingly outlasting all his friends and foes. Left to his own devices, Churchill would have been a dangerous, not to mention unstable military strategist, and the following quotation from Alan Brooke, the Chief of the Imperial General Staff, is an apt commentary: 'God knows where we would be without him, but God knows where we shall go with him.' (The War Diaries, 1939-1945 of Field Marshal Alanbrooke, Phoenix Press, 2002)

HIROSHIMA AND NAGASAKI: A NECESSARY EVIL

Although strongly opposed to the nonsense that is the arms race, a contest that nobody wins and everybody loses, I am nevertheless of the opinion that the controversial use of the atomic bomb twice in early August 1945 was a necessary evil.

There is probably more archive footage and photographs of the devastation that was inflicted on the cities of Hiroshima and Nagasaki as there is of the numerous Japanese atrocities committed in south-east Asia between 1937 and 1945. Funnily enough, those nice, civilised Japanese warriors were a bit reticent at filming their own acts of depravity. Therefore, it is all too easy to allow our emotions to wash over the harsh realities of Japanese terror and focus on the horrors of the atomic bombs. Admittedly, it is cruelly ironic that the victims of the dreaded wonder weapons were not necessarily Japanese military personnel, but women and children. In fact, it has been suggested that these two unfortunate cities were deliberately chosen by the Americans precisely because they had been relatively untouched by the Allied bombing campaign, presumably because they were of no military or strategic value. Consequently, they were nominated as ideal locations to see what the experiment of an atomic explosion would produce in a predominantly non-military population. However, this merely confirms that if truth is the first casualty of war, then civilians are frequently next in the unenviable queue.

It is necessary however to point out first of all that the Allied bombing raid on Dresden in February 1945 caused more loss of life (130,000 fatalities) than the atom bombs. Tokyo too had suffered more deaths from Allied bombs than its neighbours in Hiroshima and Nagasaki would experience. Also, for all the devastation of Hiroshima and Nagasaki, the alternative would have been an Allied invasion of Japan, assisted by the possible inclusion of the Russians, with accompanying air raids which collectively would have annihilated the Japanese islands, causing even greater loss of life both for the invaders and especially for the Japanese who had cultivated a notorious reputation of preferring to die in combat than surrender in the face of overwhelming odds.

After all, the successful American island-hopping campaign across the Pacific Ocean in preceding years had not been without inconsiderable costs, not least to the stubborn but futile Japanese resistance at the likes of Saipan and Okinawa. Above all else however, the medieval barbarity of many, though not all, Japanese troops against the Allies and especially the native peoples of south-east Asia (particularly the Chinese) was so ferocious that even the sadism of the Nazis scarcely compares. Although brutality was not confined to the Japanese, their horrific treatment of conquered peoples was such that an atomic bomb was not just necessary, but perhaps too good for them. However, it was such a shame that Emperor Hirohito was not at least forced into exile like Napoleon Bonaparte had been in 1815.

GERMANY'S SHAME

There are still thousands of elderly people in Europe (and beyond) who can testify to horrors that afflicted them and their loved ones six decades ago when it was their supreme misfortune to be in the wrong place at the wrong time. That wrong place was Nazi-occupied Europe. Many survivors and even perpetrators still shed tears and have sleepless nights when they recall the starvation in the ghettoes; the cramped conditions when herded together in cattle trucks for train journeys that extended for hundreds of miles to 'resettlement in the east' (a Nazi euphemism for death); the separation of loved ones and their subsequent disappearance from the selection ramps; the constant burning smell from chimneys; the Alsatian dogs; the death marches in sub-zero temperatures. The list of suffering is almost endless. What we conveniently forget is that hatred of Jews (gypsies, and homosexuals) was not confined to Germany. Nor is it merely a twentieth-century phenomenon. Hatred of Jews is as old as the Bible and is an international sentiment, spanning the likes of the Philistines, the Romans, the English, the French, the Russians, and even Americans. Perhaps the greatest tragedy is that today's generation prefers to ignore the lessons of the past and buries its collective head in the sand, only bringing it out to dull the senses with alcohol, James Bond movies, reality tv, and Harry Potter. Those emotional wrecks who can still recount their years of misery and pain are the lucky ones. They were reluctant students at the death camp university of hard knocks, and lived to tell the tale. It is my concern that fewer and fewer people are willing to listen and learn from them.

LITTLE BRITAIN: ***The Movie***

(featuring numerous cameo performances from a plethora of bandwagon-jumping celebrities unashamedly attempting to cash in on the show's popularity)

EIRE'S SHAME

How must Irish people feel that while millions of people worldwide sacrificed their lives or suffered in the worthy struggle against fascist tyranny in the Second World War, Eire sat out the global conflict in relative comfort. There is arguably something shameful about Eamon de Valera allowing his state to stand idly by (to coin a phrase) whilst Europe (and beyond) was ablaze. Nazism has few parallels in human history, so neutrality in a life and death struggle against this evil is perhaps an evil in itself.

Of course, 'defence lawyers' will stress the mitigating circumstances that Eire was an infant state, still learning to walk in the big wide world. It had no sizeable armed forces and its participation in the hostilities would have provoked a Luftwaffe bombing campaign against the ports of Southern Ireland. The country would almost certainly have to have been occupied by British troops for the duration of the global emergency. Herein lies the problem. The people of Eire were still nursing psychological wounds from the British response to the Easter Rising of 1916, more severely the Anglo-Irish war of independence, and the subsequent treachery of partition. Yes, with some justification, the Fianna Fail administration was not prepared to commit itself to the role of ally with the Irish people's traditional enemy – the English.

What concerns me however is that there are fanatics within the Irish republican constituency, both north and south, who still believe that centuries of British imperialism and oppression in Ireland even begins to compare with Nazi Germany's industrial waste disposal of a sizeable portion of Europe. Until Irish republicans can reconcile themselves with their next-door neighbours in Britain, the loyalists of Ulster are unlikely to be forgiving of their killing machine either. There used to be a recruitment poster from the world war which contained a family in which the children ask their father "Daddy, what did you do during the war?" This question should be addressed to the Irish nation: whilst democracies and individual liberty were seriously threatened by fascist tyranny "what did you do during the war?"

POLITICS IN NORTHERN IRELAND

The political squabbling in Norn Iron has been described accurately as 'the dialogue of the deaf', in which various parties and politicians simply wish to get their points across whilst refusing to hear their opponents' arguments and reasoning. A good friend of mine once said that it was no accident that God gave us two ears, but only one mouth, as listening is more important than talking. It is impossible to understand anything and anyone, especially your political opponents, if you do not listen. The day that Northern Ireland's motley crew of politicians choose to listen to one another's hopes and fears, or at least to respect one another's electoral mandate, is the day that the six counties joins the rest of the twenty-first century world.

Until that happy day, I would urge the struggling Ulster Unionist Party and the SDLP to consider a re-alignment with the Alliance Party in Stormont at least so as to ensure that they are the largest designated bloc. Of course, these parties have major differences over parades and post-primary selection for schoolchildren, but a Stormont coalition would allow these parties to out-flank the rejectionists and vetoists in the DUP and Sinn Fein. It has nevertheless been remarkable to find the March 2007 Assembly elections described as dull and boring. What people mean by this is the peculiar absence of drum-banging, flag-waving sectarian, tribal politics, replaced by a more sober approach to so-called bread and butter issues. Let us hope that all future elections are equally 'dull' and 'boring'! The reality is that the most irritating feature of the politicians of Northern Ireland is their constant habit of using the phrase "the reality is", but the reality is that few of them know deep down what the reality is. Personally, the reality is that the political party that removes its election posters within ten days of the conclusion of yet another tiresome election is the party that just might get my vote, though the reality is that I struggle to see the point in voting for politicians who refuse to govern, yet the reality is that Northern Ireland is crying out for locally elected politicians to take responsibility, instead of patronising one another with the parrot phrase "the reality is".

THE REALITY IS ...

Northern Ireland has belatedly followed mainland Britain in terms of spiralling house prices. With the growing surge in property values, there are now many paper millionaires in the six counties. Many recent homebuyers have discovered that their £50,000 house is now worth three or four times its previous purchase price. What baffles me is that these same individuals who have experienced good fortune are the same people who are throwing their large number of toys out of the pram whenever rates are increased and/or water charges are introduced. The disenfranchised have-nots of Ulster who cannot get so much as a toenail on the property ladder are deserving of sympathy, but it is the greedy middle-class who are vehemently protesting the introduction of water rates which might slightly dent their overseas property investment ambitions. It is hugely laughable that the very people who are opposed to increased rates and/or taxes are the same people who desire increased investment in healthcare provision and who urge the need for new roads to ease traffic congestion as they wait impatiently in their 4×4s in the traffic jams. I would like to ask the selfish middle class: how they propose we fund improved services?

Even more mischievous are the politicians who pour scorn on the flawed decision-making and imposition of new and increased taxes from Westminster and direct rule ministers. It will be fascinating in the extreme to see how Northern Irish devolution ministers intend to find the resources to finance their plethora of promises for improved services. My humble advice to any self-respecting halfwit: beware of bandwagon-jumping politicians who pledge to cut taxes and yet spend more money on improving services. How do they propose squaring this circle?

THE SAINT ANDREW'S AGREEMENT

Only in Northern Ireland are agreements not really agreements, are ceasefires not really ceasefires, deadlines are not really deadlines, peace isn't really peace, and the locally elected assembly rarely bothers to assemble, at least not locally anyway.

Nevertheless, I can exclusively reveal that the Democratic Unionist Party and Sinn Fein did conclude an agreement at St.Andrews in Scotland in the autumn of 2006, despite rumours to the contrary. Here are the terms of their pre-nuptials:

We, the Democratic Unionist Party and Sinn Fein agree the following:

We agree to disagree.

We agree to differ.

We agree to re-convene next time for multi-party talks in the Bahamas to thrash out another eleventh-hour agreement.

We agree that Stormont should continue to function as an elected assembly, which we can boycott but still get paid for.

We agree to exercise our respective vetoes when we deem appropriate.

We agree to maintain fear and mistrust in our respective communities, thereby ensuring our electoral dominance.

We agree that Snickers bars should be re-named Marathons.

We agree that 15 is the square root of 225.

We agree that Holby City is a better programme than Casualty.

We agree that 'Night Boat To Cairo' is the best-ever Madness single, unlike the SDLP who think that it is 'Our House' and the Ulster Unionists who think that it is 'House Of Fun'.

We agree that Hugo Duncan's show on Radio Ulster is better than Gerry Anderson's.

We agree that The Who should have disbanded after the death of Keith Moon.

We agree that the earth is round, subject to ratification by an extraordinary general meeting of the IRA Army Council.

We agree that Pope Benedict isn't as nice as Pope John Paul II.

We agree that orange is our favourite colour, although green is okay too.

THE BLAME GAME

If you ever wonder (or care) what the DUP and Sinn Fein will say to one another when they finally hold face-to-face talks, then imagine the following scenario. I have here published the most likely conversation between the Reverend Doctor Ian Paisley, the holy father of the Free Presbyterian Church, and Martin McGuinness, the Field Marshal of the Provisional Irish Republican Army, those brave, heroic soldiers who courageously shot people from behind and who planted bombs in shops which killed women and children. As 'the Doc' rolled a dice which produced a six, he was allowed to go first in the ensuing dialogue:

Paisley: What about all the guns that are still held in nationalist areas and all the dissident republicans?

McGuinness: What about all the guns that are still held by the loyalist paramilitaries?

Paisley: What about all the republican flags and murals in Ulster?

McGuinness: What about all the loyalist flags and murals in the six counties?

Paisley: What about the residents' groups that protest and attempt to block the road during loyalist parades?

McGuinness: What about all the contentious parades that take place in nationalist areas?

Paisley: What about all the people that have been forced into exile by the Provos?

McGuinness: What about all the people of Ireland who fled the famine and British oppression?

Paisley: What about the Protestants who have fled across the River Foyle in Londonderry?
McGuinness: What about the gerrymandering and job discrimination in Derry in the 1960s?
Paisley: What about the Northern Bank raid?
McGuinness: What about the collusion between the loyalist death squads and the British securocrats?
Paisley: What about the punishment beatings in republican areas?
McGuinness: What about the unenlightened policing of the B Specials and the RUC?
Paisley: What about the Celtic 'goal' that never crossed the line against Dunfermline in 1999?
McGuinness: What about Brian Laudrup diving in the box and winning Rangers a penalty in 1997?
Paisley: What about the Shankill bomb massacre in 1993?
McGuinness: What about the massacre at Greysteel in 1993?
Paisley: What about the persecution of Hugenots in France in the sixteenth century?
McGuinness: What about the persecution of Catholics in Elizabethan England?
Paisley: What about adjourning for tea and chocolate digestives?
McGuinness: What about having coffee and jaffa cakes instead?

Meanwhile back at the ranch, what about moving on to the next contribution of mind-expanding, intellectual brilliance?

DUP ELECTION MANIFESTO, 1987

Here follows a draft summary of the election manifesto proposals of the Democratic Unionist Party in 1987:

Sinn Fein: Smash Sinn Fein
Sharing power with fenians: Never
Talking to Sinn Fein: Never

Participating in an executive with Sinn Fein, while the IRA Army Council still exists: Never
Defence: The Ulster Defence Association
Health: Generally good, but cirrhosis of the liver is a cause for concern
Home Affairs: Affairs should be kept within the home, and dirty linen shouldn't be left hanging on the washing line for the neighbours to see
Foreign Affairs: A woman in every port
Transport: Chauffeur-driven limousines for the party leaders. Definitely no black taxis.
Education: Self-taught; unenlightened
Culture: Orange
Economy: Economical with the truth
Keeping our promises: Never
Sticking to our principles: Never

RELIGION IN NORN IRON

Roman Catholics have a thoroughly sensible approach to worship. They simply drive up to their chapels, park nearby and go in to attend Mass. However, Protestants are typically much more awkward. They like to park their cars about three miles away at an Orange Hall and spend an hour or so marching to church. In the summer, it gets extremely frustrating for motorists as Presbyterians march one way to church, Church of Ireland folk march another route to their church, and the Methodists march along a different road to their place of worship. Northern Irish people are world leaders at parading. Besides the Orange Order, there are the Apprentice Boys of Derry parades, the Royal Black Preceptory parades, the Ancient Order of Hibernian parades, Lord Mayor's parades, Boys' Brigade parades, republican parades, a Milk Cup parade, identity parades, fashion parades, and plenty more band parades. Rumour has it that the Donaghadee Chamber of Commerce and the Randalstown Horticultural Association are planning to hold annual parades. If parading was in the

Commonwealth Games, Northern Ireland would win a certain gold every time.

One word of advice, dear reader. If you ever take a taxi in Portadown to the airport, like I once mistakenly did, make sure that the driver takes you on the quickest, shortest route, unlike my chauffeur who insisted on travelling along a longer, more traditional route that his fathers and forefathers had been doing for many years! I have also discovered how difficult it is to make a telephone call to someone on the Garvaghy Road in July, as my calls always get re-routed every summer. Furthermore, when house-hunting in Norn Iron, the first question that you should address to an estate agent is " is this house on a traditional parade route?" If so, give it a wide berth, before that lovely front garden of yours is used as a public toilet each summer by 'Christian' loyalists.

LOYALIST BAND PARADES

Speaking as something of an authority on the contentious subject of loyalist parades in Northern Ireland, it is first necessary to divide parades into three different categories. Firstly, there are the major annual commemoration parades, such as the 12th of July for the Orange Order, the Relief of Derry parade for the Apprentice Boys of Derry and the Last Saturday in August demonstrations for the Royal Black Institution. Secondly, there are church parades, usually organised by the afore-mentioned groups, and finally there are band parades, which don't involve men (and women) in regalia carrying banners behind a band. The controversial Drumcree 'march', or non-march as the case may be, is actually a church parade, no more, no less. The trouble with the Irish Republican constituency, who may have aspirations of undermining or at least challenging Orange culture which tends to suffocate the life out of normality each tension-strewn summer, is that the opponents of loyalism, or those with major misgivings about parades, have been focusing their antipathy on the first two categories which are sacred to the so-called loyal orders. This approach is erroneous because it has enabled the so-called loyal orders to suggest that their routes to church worship, albeit via marching,are being threatened. If the Republican anti-loyalists had a greater modicum of sense, they would concentrate their energies on loyalist band parades.

As a witness of numerous Friday night/Saturday night band parades, I must state that these spectacles could not be further removed from Christianity, the Reformation, Protestantism, or even patriotism and loyalty to one's country. These band parades, without exception, are an unseemly display which are a far cry from Trooping The Colour or a Remembrance Day parade. Totally devoid of dignity, loyalist band parades are merely a playground for bands with paramilitary associations, led at the front by their flag party of fifteen or sixteen-year-old, gum-chewing sluts. The bandsmen are frequently ne'er-do-wells who swap their boiler suits and betting slips for some grand-looking band uniform which boosts their self-worth for a few drunken hours. They play tunes which celebrate loyalist terrorism and glorify paramilitary heroes, all belted out by a thunderous drumbeat from a semi-intoxicated drummer who wants to let the neighbourhood know that his lads are currently marching down the middle of the road, cheered on by their WKD drinking teenage hangers-on, dragging down the colours of Glasgow Rangers Football Club, which they wear. It is continuing support and public fear of these unedifying spectacles which keeps Ulster loyalism in the gutter, regrettably.

It is hugely ironic, but working-class protestants were badly neglected by the Ulster unionist bourgeois patricians in 'bygone days of yore', who failed to improve their standards of living, preferring instead to hoodwink them with the consolation that 'at least you're better than the fenians'. However, now that the 'fenians' have all the rights that they have yearned for, the increasingly neglected loyalists realise that the Orange card is not what it was cracked up to be. After all, what good is there in playing in a so-called 'Kick The Pope' band, if you are struggling to put dinner on the table for your children?

DRUMCREE

I paid my first visit to the 'trenches' at Drumcree in July 1998. It was like a scene from the battle of Naseby or Waterloo or equivalent. There was 'our lot' camped in the field with our colours and beating drums and burger vans, whilst down the road was the enemy. This was the first year that this annual farce resulted in deadlock. I knew at the time that the Orange Order had manoeuvred itself into a cul-de-sac. Unlike the previous year of 1996 when the Drumcree march was 'forced' down the Garvaghy Road, the political arithmetic at Westminster had drastically changed. In July 1996, John Major's struggling government could scarcely afford to antagonise the Unionist MPs, whose support was sometimes necessary, and so the Orangemen were dealing with a government that was favourably disposed out of political expediency, if nothing else.

By July 1998, Tony Blair was firmly ensconced in Number Ten with a landslide majority, and so the anxieties of Orangemen and/or Unionist MPs was not of primary concern to his administration. The Orange Order was now in a trap of its own making. The order expected the government to bow to their not inconsiderable pressure, but the Labour Government could afford to resist via the determination of the Parades Commission quango. I could have helpfully pointed out this logjam to the orange hierarchy, but its top brass have traditionally been patrician types who 'know best'. The trouble is that the inflexible patrician types have caused almost as much damage to their own community as the I.R.A. ever did.

THE MYTHS OF ORANGEISM

I like the joke about how William of Orange encountered King James II (his defeated foe and father-in-law) in the woods shortly after the Battle of the Boyne in July 1690 and enquired after his health. James replied that he was feeling depressed and upset after having lost the battle, only for William III to console him with the riposte "sure it will all soon be forgotten about". Members of the cross–border, Orange institution are forever bleating on about the need to safeguard their (and even others') civil liberties. What they conveniently forget is that the Boyne victory and the Glorious Revolution ushered in a century of penal laws and oppression in Ireland in which the civil and religious liberties of not only Roman Catholics but Presbyterians were curtailed by the dominant Anglican establishment.

Furthermore, dear old King Billy who is almost deified by northern Protestants was almost certainly a homosexual, who preferred the company of young men to that of his wife. Loyalists are in denial about this, but then of course, the truth hurts. It is baffling that these God-fearing Christian folk are so keen to carry banners of the mediocre William of Orange on horseback, whilst neglecting to have banners of their true saviour Jesus Christ on the cross, winning the ultimate victory at Calvary over sin and death. I get the impression that the pseudo-militarists in the loyalist community are ashamed of their semi-naked saviour on the cross at the crucifixion, preferring instead to focus on God as some kind of Field Marshal who leads his troops into battle against evil. There may be Old Testament evidence for this, but God in the guise of Jesus Christ was so much more than this – namely love for your enemies, forgiveness, compassion, humility, self-lessness, and being a good neighbour, attributes that are conspicuously absent amongst many Ulster loyalists. There is also the shocking truth that at least 10% (a very conservative estimate) of the Orange Order are members of the loyalist paramilitary organisations. To make matters worse, how must non-loyalists feel when paramilitary Orangemen and Orangemen who are serving police officers are sitting alongside each other in Orange halls? I have witnessed this.

What is more, an Orangeman pledges his allegiance to 'the rightful sovereign, being Protestant', which means that if the monarch converted to Roman Catholicism (and stranger things have happened), then the Orange Order would with-hold its support. Consequently, the Orange institution's loyalty to the throne is not unconditional, but rests upon the Head of State remaining a Protestant, and not becoming a member of the Church of Rome. Incidentally, it is amazing in the extreme that for all the slavish devotion to the British monarchy, there is not a member of the Royal Family that I am aware of who has come near an orange parade. The great, marvellous Queen finds the time and energy to visit all corners of the globe, attending a variety of social gatherings in her Commonwealth, yet she and previous monarchs have remarkably absented themselves from any orange parade. Could it be that Her Britannic Majesty agrees with much of the sentiments expressed above?

THE MYTH OF IRISH REPUBLICANISM

I actually have enormous respect for such 'bogeymen' as Gerry Adams, Martin McGuinness, Mitchel McLaughlin, and even po-faced Gerry 'Securocrats' Kelly. For all their chequered past and controversial curriculum vitae, these individuals and many others in Sinn Fein are very competent politicians, articulate, intelligent and very capable administrators. One only has to observe the increasing popularity of the Shinners in recent elections to recognise that more and more people (albeit within the Roman Catholic 'nationalist' community) respect Sinn Fein as a bona fide political party that is dedicated to representing their voters and embracing, perhaps through gritted teeth, devolved democracy in Northern Ireland.

How times are changing dramatically: the DUP contemplating sharing power with 'fenians' and Irish republicans governing the six counties from within the confines of Stormont, the bastion of Ulster unionism. One's head could be forgiven for spinning at the 'historic' turn of events in the two steps forward, one step back peace process.

My own sympathy, as a British republican, takes its cue from the socialist tradition of Irish republicanism as pioneered by Easter Rising martyr, James Connolly. I also accept that the Irish tricolour, an infamous symbol in the 'north', is as much orange as it is green, which demonstrates the apparent desire of Irish republicans to unite the erstwhile polar opposites, admittedly within the context of a thirty-two county state.

Clearly, Sinn Fein strategy is now tailored towards building confidence in the sceptical unionist community that Irish nationalists and northern loyalists can govern together, so that one fine day Protestants in the six counties will come round to the belief that sharing power in a Dublin-based government would not be such a bad thing after all, especially given the mixed record of direct rule ministers, not to mention the fact that the Roman Catholic church's stranglehold in the Republic of Ireland is much less firm than it notoriously was. Republicans could massively help their cause however by displaying a greater tolerance of parades, shedding their 'not in my backyard' territorial stance, whilst also making their own areas less of a cold house for Protestants by removing murals and flags which might render the Falls Road a tourist attraction but which collectively are not making the area very user-friendly for anyone other than Irish republicans. Both republicans and loyalists have a shared responsibility to de-militarise their territories.

What irritates me about the northern Irish republicans are the residents' groups who complain of parades in 'their' areas. Since when, did anybody or group claim ownership of an area? These 'not in my back yard' protesters may be deserving of some sympathy, given the nature of loyalist parades, but less deserving of sympathy are the Bogside Residents group, because no parade ever goes through the Bogside of Derry. Instead of which, one finds in August each year lots of arms-folded, defiant republicans standing at the Diamond in Derry in their Celtic football tops watching a parade that they despise. Where is the sense in that? If I didn't care much for the Notting Hill carnival or a St. Patrick's Day parade, I would not unnaturally stay away.

What also spoils Irish republicanism for me are the cleverdick comedians and liberal writers in England and the American-Irish who have misty-eyed perceptions of Irish republicanism. Is it no coincidence that the only major films about the conflict in Ireland, north and south, have been movies that seem to portray the poor, oppressed, loveable leprechauns of Irish republicanism suffering injustice at the hands of those big, bad, bloody, brutal British. 'Flicks' such as In The Name Of The Father, Michael Collins, and When The Wind Shakes

The Barley would have you believe that only one community has ever suffered during the conflict. I look forward to the day when the Neil Jordans of this world shoot (no pun intended) a film covering the atrocities at Ballykelly, Enniskillen, Warrenpoint, and Warrington. Yes I know that one person's terrorist is another person's freedom fighter, but there is nothing remotely glorious or heroic about exploding bombs in chip shops or shopping centres which kill women and children. Such 'freedom fighters' are on a par with paedophiles – or maybe this is an insult to child molesters.

IRISH REPUBLICANISM AND POLICING

It would be hugely inaccurate to suggest that Irish republicans don't care much for justice. However, as a movement allegedly committed to seeking justice for all the people of Ireland, Irish republicans have struggled enormously to come to terms with the need to support the administration of justice in Northern Ireland, and in particular with the obligation to sign up for policing. A quick rummage through the last century would reveal that Irish republicans have always been hostile to policing, be it in the guise of the Royal Irish Constabulary, the 'B Specials', the Royal Ulster Constabulary, and even the Police Service of Northern Ireland. The relationship between the Garda Siochana and Irish republicans could hardly be described as particularly cordial either. One could consequently be forgiven for drawing the conclusion that Irish republicans would much prefer a vigilante, wild west state. It is all very well expressing serious reservations about the neutrality of sectarian police forces imposing British law and order in the six counties, but the Irish Republican Army's own track record at policing its own community scarcely suggested the presence of a non-sectarian organisation keen on protecting the civil liberties of the individual or of the promotion of human rights.

Irish republicans like to explain away their own cavalier administration of justice by suggesting that there was a war going on, but surely does this analysis not apply to the British forces? If the Provos felt justified in bravely shooting their (sometimes unarmed) victims from behind in their dirty war, then why should the British forces be expected to treat the conflict as if it were a cricket match, with strict guidelines on fair play. The insurgency of the Irish republicans necessitated counter-insurgency from such shadowy organisations as Special Branch, the SAS, and MI5.

Gerry Adams and the Irish republican leadership are not shy at recounting their stories of brutal treatment and rough-handling in Castlereagh detention centre and elsewhere, but since when did the Provos win awards for conscientious community policing? While the European Court of Human Rights was pronouncing a guilty verdict on the British administration of justice in Northern Ireland in the 1970s, the policing practised by Irish republicans was considerably worse. 'Suspects' seized by the Provos or INLA were not read their rights, were not granted a solicitor, were not afforded a jury trial or right of appeal, and if they were lucky they were merely forced into permanent exile or shot in the knees. The unlucky ones were executed, some of whom were never to be found again and allowed a decent burial. Even dogs get a decent burial, but not victims of IRA 'policing'. With a track record like that, who are the Irish republicans to complain about injustice and to lecture everyone else about policing?

MIND YOUR LANGUAGE

Is it no coincidence that the fanatics who are campaigning for the promotion of the Irish language are the same Irish republicans who are opposed to what they perceive as 'contentious parades' and British and loyalist flags? You see, the push for greater use of the Irish language is another ploy in the process of de-Anglicisation of Ireland, north and south. Irish republicans appear to have adopted a strategy of achieving a united Ulster before they can realise a united Ireland, but their overtures of reaching out to their Protestant neighbours are being undermined by their determination to de-unionise the six counties via such initiatives as the increased provision of the Irish language in schools. Such mischief-making simply sends most members of the unionist community hurtling in the opposite direction.

It is after all the fervent hope of many Irish republicans that young northern Protestants join their Roman Catholic counterparts on an educational upbringing of Roman Catholicism, the Irish language, and Gaelic sports, so that after several years of being nourished on this diet, it is small wonder that most Ulster Roman Catholics feel no emotional attachment to anything British. You will find few Roman Catholic youngsters interested in British history or politics or say cricket. Their only 'concession' to the mainland is a fanatical devotion to that quintessential 'British' institution of Glasgow Celtic Football Club.

The trouble is that the Irish language has no shred of relevance in our changing world. Nowadays we all inhabit an international village where the likes of the far east might once appeared to be a different planet, but which is now a popular destination for western tourists, as well as an increasingly attractive market for western businesses. Is it therefore not far more important that Irish people embrace such world languages as Mandarin, or Arabic, instead of focusing on the insular, inward-looking, non-international Irish language? After all, the Irish language is of such significance on the international stage that the great ambassadors of Ireland (be it Bertie Ahern or previous premiers, Mary McAleese, Mary Robinson, Bono, Bob Geldof, Eddie O'Sullivan, Brian O'Driscoll, Steve Staunton, or Eddie Jordan) all speak English, not Irish.

The propagation of the Irish language is simply symptomatic of Sinn Fein's 'ourselves alone' siege mentality, which has no place in a Europe and world of international co-operation. More acutely, at a time when Northern Irish people are concerned about water charges, under-investment, traffic congestion, not to mention crime in the likes of west Belfast, it is staggering that Sinn Fein have their eyes on a different ball. I would venture to say that there are certain fanatical middle-class Irish republican intellectuals who have too much time on their hands.

THE DINOSAURS OF ULSTER POLITICS

I don't know whether to laugh or cry when I hear the dissident voices expressing their hostility at the political initiatives in Northern Ireland, which are paving the foundations for the DUP sharing power with Sinn Fein and with Irish republicans supporting the administration of law and order. On the one extreme, the Reverend Doctor Ian Paisley, the Pope of the Free Presbyterian Church, has come under fire from Protestant bigots who simply cannot entertain the prospect of power-sharing with the great unwashed heretics of the church of Rome. They disguise their hatred with the age-old concern about sitting round a table with terrorists.

On the other extreme are the unreconstructed republicans who wish to have 'no British presence in Ireland'. Do they not realise that there is a British presence everywhere, that there is an Irish presence in Britain? They sound uncannily like citizens of the deep south who want no black presence in the American Congress, like Nazis who want no Jewish presence in Europe, and the National Front who want no Asian presence in Britain. Do these republican racists want no Polish, or Romanian, or Czech presence in Ireland either? What about the Vietnamese; are they as unwelcome as the British?

Perhaps the Soviet Union had the right idea about dissidents: to lock them up in mental hospitals. Irish republicans who are opposed to the PSNI are basically members of the DUP – the dinosaurs of Ulster politics.

BIGOTRY

I recently heard Top Cat himself, gorgeous George Galloway, referring to certain 'Orange' Protestant citizens of Glasgow as bigots. I have previously heard Northern Irish Orangemen being described as bigots, as well as the anti-abortion lobby, not to mention members of the far right. However, bigot is a term that applies to anyone who holds such strong views that he or she refuses to tolerate any contrary opinion. Surely therefore, 'bigot' could be used as a label for those implacably opposed to the Orange Order, as well as the pro-abortion lobby, not to mention members of the far left. In fact, when you think about it, there is a bit of the bigot in all of us, and you don't have to be a big-mouthed Alf Garnett, with a fear of 'darkies', to be a bigot. Perhaps bigotry is like beauty. It's in the eye of the beholder, eh George?

GORGEOUS GEORGE GALLOWAY

I feel that I must pay tribute to a man who is fast becoming Britain's top politician, Top Cat himself, Mr George Galloway MP. I don't agree by all means with all of Galloway's politics, but one cannot help but admire a man who polarises public opinion like virtually no other. Nobody, it seems, sits on the fence when asked about gorgeous George. I for one enjoyed the way he ran rings around several wet-behind-the-ears Congressmen. Furthermore, his appearance on Celebrity Big Brother may have been dismissed in some quarters as a grotesque publicity stunt, but larger than life Galloway was merely enabling Joe Public the opportunity to view an elected politician without the usual trappings of shirt, tie, briefcase and despatch box. Galloway courageously wanted to be seen as he really is: drinking beverages, munching food, and squabbling with fellow-housemates in an effort to humanise the public perception of a politician.

Other politicians and commentators choose to pour scorn on Top Cat's Big Brother antics, but have we not grown wearily accustomed to revelations about the extra-curricular, recreational activities of many of our holier-than-thou, moralising politicians. Judging by the behaviour and lifestyle behind closed doors of some of our politicians, it is refreshing to find Galloway reveal himself, 'warts and all', on television 24/7 for a few weeks.

Speaking as an underdog myself, I respect Mr Galloway's support for the underdog, but I wonder if his championing of the cause of

British Muslims is an act of political expediency, borne out of the fact that Muslims form a significant proportion of his Bethnal Green constituency. Galloway will probably retort that he chose to stand for parliament in a predominantly Muslim area because he has major sympathies with the causes of Palestinians, Iraqis, and British immigrants. If he were to be elected for Westminster from a 'shire' constituency, would Mr Galloway still devote so much time to sympathising at length for British immigrants on his Talksport radio shows?

Mr Galloway and I have different religious backgrounds and our football sympathies are for different Glasgow football teams. Nevertheless, one cannot help but admire this principled politician who has probably succeeded the great Tony Benn as the darling of that most endangered of species – the British Left. In a modern political landscape where catch-all politicos campaign for the disenfranchised whilst being in league with big business, Galloway is a one-off. If nothing else, Mr Galloway is one of only a handful of politicians who is recognisable, unlike the Labour cabinet ministers who have only temporarily grown a spine and emerged from their trenches to jockey in behind one or two candidates in the race to succeed Bambi and Thumper.

However, I would like him to answer, whether or not a future Palestine state or current Islamic state (take your pick) would be willing to entertain a twice weekly show where the host pours scorn on their respective foreign policy. Mr Galloway should count his blessings that he lives in a country where his right to criticise British and American foreign policy twice weekly is permitted. Would such a show be tolerated in an Islamic state?

THE OLD FIRM

Judging by the number of Irish tricolours paraded at Parkhead once a fortnight throughout each winter, I would argue that Glasgow Celtic's biggest claim to fame is that they are the first Irish club, and not British club, to win the coveted European Cup in Lisbon in 1967. I have always been baffled as to why so many English people (and non-celts) have had a love affair with Celtic. Has nobody ever told them that certain sections of Celtic Park have been known to sing anti-British, Irish republican songs? As a Hun (quite clearly) I am perpetually disappointed that Glasgow Rangers are viewed as the epitome of sectarianism while Glasgow Celtic fans are portrayed as loveable leprechauns. Perhaps Rangers are simply not very good at public relations, which I suspect, in spite of possessing two excellent ambassadors in the guise of Walter Smith and the hugely personable Ally McCoist. Could it be that the Ibrox club has been demonised for its' former policy of employing only Protestants on their playing staff? It is also a real tragedy for Glasgow Rangers that their January 1971 Ibrox disaster at the end of an Old Firm clash did not earn the club the massive outpouring of international sympathy that Liverpool and Manchester United have successfully derived from the Hillsborough and Munich tragedies of 1989 and 1958 respectively. Even the understandable exuberance demonstrated by inebriated but harmlessly happy Rangers fans at the pitch-invasion conclusion of their team's 1972 European Cup Winners' Cup triumph prompted a year's ban, denying the club the opportunity to defend their hard-earned trophy. It seems historically like Celtic can do no wrong, and big bad Glasgow Rangers can do no right.

As a Hun, I can acknowledge the football skills of the likes of the late Jimmy Johnstone, Kenny Dalglish, and the 'colourful' Paolo di Canio, but again there is a half-truth that only the green half of Glasgow is truly dedicated to playing entertaining football. Has nobody ever seen or heard of the likes of Jim Baxter, Willie Henderson, the late Davie Cooper, Brian Laudrup, and of course Paul Gascoigne?

Such is the ferocity of emotion aroused by an Old Firm contest that even if Rangers and Celtic played each other in pre-season, the match couldn't be labelled a 'friendly'. The irony is that the management and playing staff of each club have had a healthy respect for one another more often than not, but on the terraces the auld historical and religious differences still guarantee a unique, mutual hostility. As for the contentious issue of bragging rights, well, the Hoops not surprisingly remind us of their European success, albeit in a year when even Linfield from Northern Ireland were narrowly beaten in the quarter-finals, which is hardly a barometer of strong competition. Gers fans point to their club's world record number of league championship titles, admittedly in a league devoid of many realistic contenders. The tragedy of Scottish football is that each member of the Old Firm will struggle massively to repeat the successes of the 1960s and early 1970s when the blues and greens were heavyweight contenders on the European stage, whilst nowadays they are also-rans.

MERSEY MISERY

Liverpool football fans like to taunt Chelsea Football Club for having 'no history'. This is a ludicrous remark because Chelsea, like all football clubs and other organisations, does have a history. What is much more valid is if Kopites boast that their own history is more triumphant than that of Chelsea, or almost anyone for that matter. Anfield has been blessed with the expert management of Bill Shankly and then Bob Paisley, not to mention such footballing greats as Kevin Keegan, Kenny Dalglish, Alan Handsome, and Ian Rush, to name but a few. However, it has not all been wine and roses for Liverpool, as the club remains somewhat traumatised by the disasters at Heysel in Brussels in May 1985 and at Hillsborough in Sheffield in April 1989.

What irritates me about the red half of Merseyside is its refusal to accept any responsibility for the catastrophes in the European Cup Final followed by the tragedy of the FA Cup semi-final. Liverpool Football Club supporters would have you believe that they are wholly blameless, and holy righteous. It is all symptomatic of a club whose supporters' devotion is akin to religious fervour and thus ensures that Liverpool Football Club is a Vatican-like institution that is apparently infallible and above criticism.

Equally baffling for me is that Liverpool have absorbed much neutral support and affection even though the violent actions of a minority of its fans in May 1985 resulted in a ban on all English clubs competing in Europe for several years. Silly Arsenal supporters ought to realise that it was Liverpool fans, and not Chelsea or Tottenham Hotspur, that prevented their team from making a well-earned attempt to compete in the European Cup in 1989. Everton fans are only too painfully aware of the consequences of this ban on English clubs as their "small club" were also denied the opportunity to compete in the European Cup in 1985 and 1987 because of the violence of some Liverpool followers in May 1985. It must be the equivalent of being punished for something that your next-door neighbour did!

The well-oiled propaganda machine of Anfield, fuelled by a disproportionately high presence of Scousers and ex-Liverpool players on BBC football, Radio Five Live, and Blokesport insist that the ninety-six martyrs of Hillsborough died exclusively from police negligence. Whatever the truth, Liverpool football supporters think that they have the monopoly on suffering. Their morality is laughable. Scornful of the foreign owners of certain other football clubs, Liverpool were so opposed to this development that they proceeded to sell their red soul and do likewise. Perhaps that nice Boris Johnson was right: Liverpudlians do take pleasure in cultivating their own sense of 'misery'.

IN DEFENCE OF CHELSEA FOOTBALL CLUB

This is my book, and I will write what I want to. I promised myself that I would avoid a discourse on the merits of Chelsea Football Club, but hey-ho. If you are a non-Chelsea person who lacks exquisitely sophisticated taste in football teams, you are welcome to take the advice of the television newsreader and look away if you don't want to see the results.

I actually had the deep misfortune to start enduring the fluctuating fortunes of Chelsea in the mid-1970s when they were a spectacularly under-achieving mid-table Second Division outfit, managed by the admirable Eddie McCreadie. So let's get one thing straight folks: I ain't no gold-digger.

Next half-truth that requires demolition is the nonsense that without our Siberian sugar daddy, Roman Abramovich, Chelsea would be the mediocrities of yesteryear. Sorry ladies and gentlemen, but were it not for the untimely death of Chelsea benefactor Matthew Harding in a helicopter crash in October 1996, then west London's finest would have challenged the duopoly of Manchester United and Arsenal several years sooner, given that Mr Harding was one of Britain's richest men whose wealth had already facilitated the arrival of such superstars as Ruud Gullit, Mark Hughes, Gianluca Vialli, Roberto di Matteo, and Frank Leboeuf.

It was always inevitable that Chelsea would acquire the necessary resources to challenge for honours, given that some of the locals and some of the fans are not short of a bob or two, not least the dozens of showbiz supporters of London's most glamorous football club. In fact, as far back as 1930, newly-promoted Chelsea flashed the cash to buy the Newcastle legend Hughie Gallacher and a few other Anglo-Scottish internationals such as Alec Jackson, the Gay Cavalier. Even the post-war signing of England centre-forward Tommy Lawton did not herald an era of triumph. One could go on, but hopefully you get the picture. Thus, for all the big spending long before Mr Abramovich was even born, Chelsea remained adrift of success, waiting until 1967 to appear in a Wembley FA Cup final and a further thirty years to win an FA Cup final at the twin towers, whilst one paltry league championship triumph in the club's first 99 years was scant reward for a club recognised as a sleeping giant.

Fast forward to the victorious year of 2005, the club's centenary, and I was dismayed by the abuse, bitterness and jealousy heaped on the club. Such hostility was conspicuously absent during decades of failure, so one can only assume that Chelsea became so frighteningly successful that their glory upset several football fans. After all, who worries about the on-field and off-field behaviour of a mid-table club? Nevertheless, I was especially disappointed by the begrudging reactions of Arsenal supporters. For many of the north London riff-raff, Chelsea were a likeable bunch of losers led by that nice Mr Ranieri who only started to go off the straight and narrow when they had the bad manners to knock Arsenal out of the Champions League, robbing the Gooners of their best-ever chance of lifting European club football's greatest prize. Many Chelsea fans have acknowledged that the Arsenal 'invincibles', so-called, of 2004 played eye-catching football. It was a real shame that Gooners failed to reciprocate by respecting Chelsea's back-to-back triumphs. After a decade of avoiding league defeats against Chelsea, one might think that Arsenal followers might be a bit more generous. Instead of which, the media-fuelled vitriol has simply created a siege mentality at Stamford Bridge which seems certain to forge further success, even if the club continues to slide down the popularity table.

The double-standards in English football over the last decade have caused me to laugh. For example, Chelsea were criticised for employing a foreign manager. Arsenal were so outraged by Chelsea appointing Ruud Gullit that shortly afterwards they recruited that nice English chap, Monsieur Arsene Wenger in 1996. Chelsea were then screamed at for fielding a team without a single English player. Arsenal were so incensed by this that they have recently done likewise. Recently, we have been vilified for dipping into the bottomless pockets of a foreign investor. Aston Villa, Manchester United, West Ham United, Portsmouth and Liverpool have been so disgusted by this that they have done, guess what, the same. Perhaps imitation is merely a form of flattery. It seems apparent that where Chelsea lead, the others follow, selling their moralising souls in the process. For any football supporter who speculates about what his club will be doing in five years from now, he or she only has to observe what Chelsea are doing at present. Yes folks, Chelsea are the leaders in more ways than one.

One question remains unanswered. Are Chelsea really guilty of all the unsolved crimes in human history, or could it be that the supporters of one or two football clubs are crying like infants because that big bad wolf, Jose Mourinho has taken their 'toys' away from them. I'll let you decide.

THE SPECIAL ONE

Nobody it seems has a 'neutral' opinion of Jose Mourinho. Seldom has a non-sportsman impacted on British sport to such a controversial extent. Depending upon whether or not you are a follower of Chelsea Football Club, Jose Mourinho is either regarded as an arrogant, egotistical, unpleasant, self-important megalomaniac (obviously well-suited to the world of football) or else he is a refreshing breath of air to a football landscape where Mr Ferguson and Mr Wenger ruled the 'manor' like a couple of Kray brothers who tolerate no competitors on their patch.

Mourinho's love –hate relationship with the British public perhaps made the worst possible start when he had the bare-faced cheek to lead FC Porto to success in the 2003 UEFA Cup Final against that nice Martin O'Neill's loveable Glasgow Celtic. Mourinho then had the audacity the following year to jump for joy at Old Trafford when FC Porto condemned Sir Alex and his little team to an early exit from the Champions League. As if this all was not bad enough, Mr Mourinho at his first Chelsea press conference dared to describe himself as 'special', a piece of self-analysis based on Mourinho's success at transforming European also-rans FC Porto not only into the best team in his native Portugal, but into UEFA Cup champions and Champions League winners in successive seasons. Although the word 'special' seems therefore perfectly appropriate, the trouble is that in Britain, the press and public are historically not favourably disposed to people who dare to call themselves 'special'. Thereafter, Mourinho was labelled 'the special one' by the press. It was always going to be a difficult moniker to live up to.

To be honest, Mourinho is an unpredictable loose cannon, who has a flair for 'foot in mouth' remarks. Amongst other things, he denounced a visiting Tottenham team for earning a 0-0 draw at Stamford Bridge by 'parking a bus' in front of his team's goal, a tactic perfected by Mourinho's own FC Porto. Mourinho then went on to embark in a public war of words with Frank Rijkard of Barcelona, accusing the Catalans' boss of chatting to the referee at half-time in a crucial Champions League match. Sir Alex Ferguson received a similar accusation following a League Cup semi-final at Stamford Bridge. Mourinho's most notorious spat however has been with Arsenal's agent provocateur, Arsene Wenger, who was labelled a voyeur who frequently used a telescope to focus on the activities of Chelsea Football Club. To be fair to Mourinho, Monsieur Wenger seemed to be commenting on the merits or otherwise of Chelsea on what seemed like a daily basis with Mourinho claiming that Chelsea Football Club had compiled a dossier full of Wenger's rent-a-quote remarks. Finally, there was the goal-keeping near tragedies at Reading in October 2006 where Mourinho all but robbed his club of temporary sympathy by suggesting that Petr Cech's near-fatal injury was no accident, while also calling into question the efficiency of the emergency services.

My two abiding memories of Mourinho feature firstly throwing his winner's medal into the crowd after his team had secured their second consecutive Premiership trophy. Whether 'the special one' was rewarding the Chelsea faithful or expressing his contempt for the football league, only he knows. However, this was eclipsed by the pre-match press conference when Mourinho brazenly named the Barcelona starting line-up on the eve of a Champions League encounter. As a piece of pure theatre it ranks alongside that other 'special one' Brian Clough when ol' big head ran onto a football field and manhandled a pitch invader.

In Mourinho's defence, he reserves the right to stand up for his team and football club against the tirade of bitterness and jealous abuse that has been showered on Mourinho and Chelsea. People scoff that anybody could successfully manage a squad of superstars, but admire him or loathe him, Jose Mourinho is the most compelling manager in British football since Brian Clough.

ARSENE WENGER: DIGNIFIED IN DEFEAT

Arsene Wenger has guided the fortunes of Arsenal Football Club's quest for glory for more than ten years. During this time, Monsieur Wenger has not only transformed this club of one-nil merchants of pragmatic football into a team of eye-catching total footballers, but he has presided over two domestic doubles, three Premiership titles, four FA Cup triumphs, and a near-miss in the Champions League. Perhaps only Herbert Chapman in the 1930s can begin to rival Wenger's record of distinction in north London.

Nevertheless, while Arsenal fans are quick to join in the chorus of Jose Mourinho is an arrogant ... , Arsene Wenger is infinitely more arrogant, not to mention snooty. Wenger never ceases to pour scorn on an opposing team that dares to defend properly against his. He feels that he is so superior to other managers that he cannot even give them eye contact when he reluctantly shakes their hand at the end of a football match. I think that Mr Wenger spends the whole of a football match dreading the prospect of the post-match hand-shake, feeling that his opposite number is so inferior that Wenger should only shake him with a barge pole. At least, the other managerial bogeymen, Sir Alex and Mourinho are much more gracious. Mourinho frequently embraces his opposite number at the end of the proceedings while Mr Ferguson is not averse to a bit of post-match banter with the other manager as they walk off together towards the tunnel. Also, for all the success at Arsenal, they have also lost occasionally during the Wenger era. On this page, I have compiled in full the occasions when Monsieur Wenger (or Whinger) has conceded that the other team deserved to win and that the opposing team played good football.

GORMLESS GOONERS

Arsenal supporters would have you believe that they have the best manager in the Premiership (in spite of his touchline tantrums), the best centre forward in the league, the best midfielder in the Premiership, and the quickest centre half partnership in the Premiership, not to mention the best youth policy, the best stadium, and no doubt the most superior corner flags and goal-posts. Before Cashley Cole had the good taste to move across to west London, Arsenal also boasted that they had the best left-back in England. Well, if they are this good, then why have they failed to win the Premiership for the third successive season, as well as staring at the likelihood of failing to win any silverware for the second year in succession?

THE JANUARY TRANSFER WINDOW

A frenzy of transactions has greeted the opening of the football transfer window. Manchester United have poached Bolton Wanderers' coach driver, Tommy Sexton, in a frantic effort to ensure that the team arrives on time for their visit to the City Of Manchester Stadium. Sexton's four hour dash to Portsmouth last season with the Bolton team was cited as the impressive performance which caught the attention of the Glazer family, not to mention several speed cameras. Chelsea meanwhile have exchanged Michael Ballack for an armchair, thus enabling Roman Abramovich to actually sit down during a match. Furthermore, Andriy Shevchenko has been loaned out to Stockport County until the rest of the season. Tottenham Hotspur have also been busy in the January sales, successfully persuading AC Milan's Brazilian assistant groundsman, Roberto Romario, to join as cover for the ground staff's Romanian prodigy, Mircea Ceacescu, who will be absent for five weeks with torn ligaments, missing in particular the difficult FA Cup third round home tie against Dagenham And Redbridge. Rafael Benitez is reportedly off to Spain in mid-January to sign Sergio Garcia, Jose-Maria Olazabal, and Rafael Nadal. Back in London, Arsene Wenger has dismissed growing speculation that he intends to sign English ticket-office worker Billy Brooking from West Bromwich Albion, claiming that the last thing that the Emirates Stadium requires is any English riff-raff about the place. Newcastle United's attempts to waste more money have been thwarted by the club's insistence that any new signing undergo five medical examinations to ensure that they don't purchase damaged goods again. Leeds United are rumoured to be signing Zinedine Zidane, Ruud Gullit, and Marco Van Basten in a desperate attempt to arrest the club's slide towards the Conference. There are also unconfirmed reports that Everton are tapping up a seven year-old paper boy from Tranmere. Watch this space for any more breaking news and further developments.

THE MYTH OF SIR ALF RAMSEY

In recognition of England's historic triumph in the 1966 World Cup finals, Alf Ramsey was knighted and forever held, it seems, in the highest esteem. Dare I say it, but England won football's biggest tournament by default. The usual suspects, Brazil and Italy, went absent during the finals competition, and the host nation merely profited from the absence of any worthy challengers. England actually started the tournament by failing to score in a Wembley fixture for the first time since a 1–0 defeat by Scotland as far back as 1938. Furthermore, for all their energy and industry, the World Cup winners were hardly over-flowing with flair, skill, or imagination. They were simply the best of a bad bunch.

However, far from building upon English football's finest two hours, 'Sir Alf' guided England back to mediocrity with under-achievement in the European Championships of 1968 and 1972, and a slightly premature exit from the 1970 World Cup finals when the reigning champions allowed a semi-final place to slip from their fingers after Ramsey mistakenly replaced Bobby Charlton with Colin Bell, and West Germany were able to achieve the mother of all comebacks, with a 3-2 win after extra-time.

Notwithstanding allowing West Germany to pluck victory from the jaws of defeat, the greatest indictment of Sir Alf was that this 'great man' failed to ensure qualification for the 1974 finals in West Germany for a country that had been world champions a few years earlier. What was really criminal was that Ramsey had the talent at his disposal, but this bloody-minded individual consistently neglected to choose his country's most gifted players in favour of solid but unspectacular team players. Thus, when English football needed (and actually had) skilful footballers who could change the course of a match, Sir Alf refused to entertain the selection of such prodigies as Charlie George, Alan Hudson, and Peter Osgood, while even Rodney Marsh was only rewarded with nine caps. Whilst Holland emerged as the standard-bearers of total football, dedicated to playing with skill, Ramsey was plotting a course of no-nonsense football, which proved to be a nonsense strategy. As a consequence of Ramsey's neglect of talent, England were denied their place on football's biggest stage on an infamous night at Wembley in October 1973 when a Polish goal-keeper, dismissed as a 'clown' by Brian Clough, proceeded to make a fool of an England team that had actually scored seven goals without reply only three weeks earlier at home to Austria. What summed up the mindset of Sir Alf was when he needed a spark to rescue the deadlock against Poland, the manager called for 'Kevin' to warm up as a replacement. As the great Kevin Keegan prepared to unzip his track-suit top, he was told that no it was the less talented Kevin Hector who was being summoned at England's hour of need. The rest is history.

England had now slipped well and truly down into mediocrity, failing to compete in a World Cup finals for a further eight and a half years, which was truly ironic when one considers that English clubs were hugely successful in the three European club competitions throughout the 1970s, yielding no fewer than three winners of the European Cup, two successes in the European Cup Winners' Cup, and five UEFA Cup winners. If the great 'Sir Alf' was such a success, then how did he allow a country with so many skilful players to fade from the summit of world football?

ENGLAND WILL WIN THE NEXT FOOTBALL WORLD CUP

I was never comfortable with the appointment of Ericsson as England football team manager. Surely Nokia or Samsung would have been better choices. Anyhow, debate rages on in bars about who have been England's best-ever players. Personally, I think that the three best strikers in England since the last world war have been Joe Gormley, Derek 'Red Robbo' Robinson and Arthur Scargill. In my humble estimation, these strikers have been more prolific than Jimmy Greaves, Geoff Hurst, or Alan Shearer. Opinion also remains divided on who have been England's best left-wingers in recent years, but I believe that nobody comes close to Anthony Wedgwood Benn. Tony Blair started out as a promising left-winger, but after moving over to the centre, he now prefers to play on the right nowadays. On the right wing, Mrs Thatcher has been very 'effective', surpassing even the great David Beckham whose glittering reputation is based on his delivery of crosses, but nobody has ever managed to make as many crosses as the Romans used to do.

When England toiled recently in Germany against the mighty Paraguay, the supremely talented Trinidad And Tobago and against the awesome Costa Rica, we were informed that the poor dears could not cope with the heat. Only weeks before, we were all assured that England were champions-elect, yet it now appears that any possible England success at the World Cup finals is at the mercy of the temperatures. However, is it not the case that almost every World Cup in recent memory, perhaps with the obvious exception of the 1966 World Cup in sunny England is played in hot, summery weather? How then do England propose to win a World Cup played in hot weather? A recent home humiliation at the hands of Spain was played in freezing February in freezing Manchester, so I would venture to suggest that England cannot play in cold weather either. Perhaps England's best chance of future glory in the World Cup is if the tournament is played indoors as a five-a-side competition.

I have no doubts whatsoever that England will finally emulate their success of 1966, if the following is realised: penalty kicks are banned, Portugal and Sweden fail to qualify for the World Cup finals, and the following are disqualified during the tournament: Argentina, Brazil, France, Germany, Holland, Italy, and Spain.

THE BEAUTIFUL GAME

With greedy footballers, egged on by parasite agents, demanding ever higher amounts of wages and the soccer supporter required to cover the increase via extortionate rises in ticket prices, the beautiful game is in danger of losing its charm. As a football observer with more brain cells than most tabloid sports reporters put together, I propose the following cosmetic surgery.

The number of international matches that England play in a year should be twelve (including competitive games), averaging out at one fixture every month. The debacle at home to Spain in February 2007 painfully reminded England football followers of the folly of friendlies. What we find increasingly are opportunities for fringe players to stake their claims, but where is the value in substituting Steven Gerrard at half-time? Would Brazil replace Ronaldinho at half-time or Argentina have played Diego Maradona for merely 45 minutes? Would England rugby team substitute Jonny Wilkinson at half-time? Friendlies are farces, because as Glenn Hoddle amongst others discovered, international players were sometimes unfit to play and yet like Wayne Rooney, they were remarkably available a few days later to perform for their club. As long as the national coach is cavalier with his team selections, club managers get cross about releasing players to represent their country, and footballers continue to pick and choose which internationals they want to play in, friendlies will remain half-hearted, joke fixtures.

Speaking of fixtures, there are far too many matches in a season. This observation is as obvious as the nose on one's face. How can England ever expect to perform, if individuals such as Steven Gerrard and the super-fit Frank Lampard are required to play half a dozen pre-season friendlies, about fifty league and cup club matches both domestic and European, and then at least a dozen internationals on top of this. Something has got to give. Sixty or seventy playing commitments in a season is idiocy in the extreme for any professional footballer. What England is crying out for is a Premier League that is trimmed to eighteen or better still sixteen teams, thereby easing fixture congestion during Christmas and the new year, enabling the best clubs to do themselves justice in European competitions, and ridding the Premiership of the handful of clubs each season who provide nothing more than nuisance value. Relegation and promotion can still take place, with two teams each swapping one league for another. Of course, many Premiership football chairmen, fearful of the potential trapdoor of relegation, will dismiss any proposal to cut the size of the Premier League, as agreeing to do so would be akin to the proverbial turkeys voting for Christmas. However, as long as selfish football clubs dictate their terms and conditions, England's best players will be weighed down with too many football fixtures. I find it frankly remarkable that club comes before country, which explains England's habitual under-achievement in major tournaments.

Finally, I would humbly suggest that the European Champions League be re-structured. The current format of eight groups of four teams is frequently as competitive as a race between a horse and a tortoise. We should have four groups of eight teams, with two qualifiers each reaching the quarter-finals. Of course, it means seven group games with some teams playing four home matches and others playing three, but at least the pre-Christmas Champions League would be more exciting and less of a procession for all the top teams, with less margin for error. Football, in my humble opinion, needs such a facelift to preserve its beauty.

THE TIMES THEY ARE A-CHANGIN'

Anything is possible and miracles do happen. Consider the following: Moses and the Israelites crossing the sea on foot; Daniel surviving his stint in the lion's den; Jesus Christ walking on water and then rising from the dead; victory at Rorke's drift; the deliverance of Dunkirk; the collapse of communism; the crumbling of the Berlin Wall; Nelson Mandela becoming President of South Africa; England winning the rugby World Cup; Chelsea winning the Premiership (oh alright, buying it then); England winning the Ashes; a Scotsman playing tennis at Wimbledon; Ireland rugby team ranked third in the world. Whatever next, might I speculate? Perhaps Arsenal winning the Champions League, Liverpool winning the Premiership, Newcastle United winning silverware, or Tottenham Hotspur qualifying for the Champions League, or even maybe I will have sex ... with a woman.

ASHES TO ASHES

As an ardent follower of the England cricket team (albeit from my own living room), I have been staggered by yet another ritual capitulation in another Ashes series when those nice, modest Australians have simply trounced our hapless bunch. The 2006 series has been the cricketing equivalent of a two-horse race in which one horse is two or three fences ahead of its rival. It has been that cringe-worthy.

It ought to have been so much different. Firstly, the history of sport is inundated with examples of an inferior team or competitor overcoming the odds to triumph against their apparent superiors. Of course we all acknowledge through gritted teeth that the Aussies have more talented players, but since when have all sporting contests been decided in favour of the most talented participant? Cricket, like many sports, is as much about the mind as it is about pure ability, and it is in the mind that the England cricket team have been a monumental (no pun intended) disappointment.

For a start, I have been appalled to find England batsmen, particularly Strauss and Bell, and even Pietersen and Flintoff, smiling frequently whilst at the crease. Oh yes we can claim that this is the age-old English trait of smiling in the face of adversity, but far from being a gesture of defiance, it is merely an act of stupidity. You won't find Australian batsmen grinning from ear to ear, even when they are humiliating England's mediocre bowlers. Far from it. The likes of Justin Langer and Ricky Ponting might have been reaping a plentiful harvest of runs against England's inept bowlers, but any pleasure that they derived was not obvious. Andrew Symonds in plundering over 150 runs en route to his maiden test century in Melbourne looked like he was at a funeral service, whilst Ponting was furious with himself for being dismissed at Brisbane for a paltry 190-plus. The Aussies may be cocky and arrogant off the pitch, but they are deadly serious on it. England need to take a leaf out of their book. You will struggle to find archive material of Allan Border, Glen Chappell, Ian Chappell, or Steve Waugh smiling their way through an innings. The great Geoffrey Boycott, a worthy adversary of the likes of the terrible twins Dennis Lillee and Jeff Thomson, once remarked that a batsman should not smile until he has returned to the pavilion – with a hundred to his name.

Speaking of returning to the pavilion, I am stunned to find England's top order batsmen soaking up the sun on the dressing-room balcony in their tee-shirt and shorts, reading a newspaper without a care in the world, not long after having been dismissed for yet another puny score. A batsman who fails to make a double-figure score should be ordered off to the nets for much-needed practice, instead of posing in sunglasses on the pavilion balcony. England looked yet again like a bunch of holiday-makers going through the motions, while their opponents played hard with the kind of focus that world-class professionals exude. England need to toughen up their act quite drastically as it was abundantly clear that whilst one team wanted to win, the other eleven were desperate to win. Facts have clearly underpinned this obvious difference in emphasis.

England have to start thinking outside of the box for a change. Habitual gestures such as the team huddle or Celtic 'prayer meeting' as I regard it, fool no-one. Where is the benefit of a team huddle at the start of a day's play if at the end of it, your opponents are an embarrassing 360 for 3 as on Day One of the Ashes series? I would suggest that any fielder who drops a catch be ordered to buy the bowler a pint at the end of the day. The trouble is that a few England bowlers could potentially end up with a hangover when they take to the field the following day. England, in my opinion, have an abundance of good batsmen, with the likes of Marcus Trescothick, Michael Vaughan, Mark Butcher, Robert Key, Owais Shah, Mark Ramprakash, Ed Joyce, and Anthony McGrath not even involved in the Ashes debacle.

It is however the bowling department that demands emergency surgery. The vastly over-rated Steve Harmison rarely looks like accumulating a five-wicket haul, and I will never know why Harmison has always been awarded the benefit of the doubt while Chris Silverwood was criminally overlooked after a promising start to his test career included a 5 for 91 in Cape Town against a strong South African team in 1999. Ultimately, the England cricketers whose reputations have been enhanced after the whitewash series of 2006 are the likes of Vaughan and sicknote Simon Jones, because it was their 'good fortune' not to be involved in another Ashes funeral of English cricket. I also am perplexed that nobody seems responsible or willing to take responsibility for the Ashes catastrophe. We have been informed that the lack of early match preparation was not to blame, the captain, Andrew Flintoff, was not to blame, and even the coach, Duncan Fletcher, was not to blame. Excuse me, but when you are trounced 5-0, I would venture to suggest that it does not happen by pure chance. Surely it is time to recruit Mike Gatting, Graham Gooch, Nasser Hussain, or Martin Moxon as England coach. I personally blame a dreadful opening partnership and a very ordinary bowling attack, Hoggard and Panesar excepted, as well as the obvious factor of poor selections, although whether any one is man enough to accept responsibility remains to be seen, eh Mr Fletcher, eh Mr Graveney?

THE WARS OF THE ROSES

The fifteenth century conflict between the royal houses of Lancaster and York gets re-enacted every summer in less bloody circumstances in the north of England when the red rose of Lancashire and the white rose of Yorkshire do battle on the cricket field. It is probably English county cricket's nearest thing to a grudge match, although the rivalry is less hostile than say its footballing equivalent of Leeds United versus Manchester United.

As a Yorkie, I grew up with the unusual boast (and family joke) that I stood more chance of being selected for Yorkshire than the likes of Richard Hadlee, Michael Holding or Viv Richards, not because of superior cricketing talent, but because the county recruited its players only on the basis that they were Yorkshire-born. A personal highlight of mine was paying a visit to the hallowed turf of The Oval to witness an excellent Yorkshire team trounce Surrey by nine wickets in a Benson and Hedges quarter-final in May 1996. A young prodigy by the name of Michael Vaughan was amongst the runs in the visitors' triumph that day. I too marked the occasion with a semi-inebriated pitch invasion at the successful conclusion of the proceedings, whereupon I attempted with mixed results to engage in conversation with such test cricketers as Michael Bevan, Alec Stewart, Graham Thorpe, and Craig White.

The scene was now set for unarguably one of the greatest-ever domestic one-day contests when Yorkshire crossed the Pennines to engage in a semi-final against the old enemy. Rain delays decreed that the Old Trafford battle would need a second day to complete the match and in the event, the Tykes recovered from losing five wickets before 100 had even been posted on the scoreboard to set the home team a target of 250, courtesy of an unbroken sixth wicket stand between Michael Bevan and former England wicket-keeper, Richard Blakey. The hosts in reply suffered the early loss of Michael Atherton to a fired-up Darren Gough, whose animated celebration of the England skipper's wicket owed something to his exclusion from the national team at that particular time. The red rose continued to wilt, losing wickets at regular intervals, but just when all seemed lost, future England wicket-keeper, Warren Hegg, proceeded to pluck victory from the jaws of defeat with a remarkable innings. It took a two off the very last ball of the match to clinch the narrowest possible victory for Lancashire. I regard this twentieth-century Battle of Bosworth as second only to Chelsea's unlucky exit at the hands of Liverpool in a Champions League semi-final as my most heart-breaking sporting memory.

Lightning would strike twice when Lancashire overcame Yorkshire in another close semi-final encounter a couple of months later. In fact, for several years an outstanding Yorkshire team had an unfortunate knack of losing in the quarter-finals and semi-finals of one-day competitions, just when glory beckoned. Then, when the Tykes finally achieved a place in a Lords final in 1999, after a twelve-year wait, they were comprehensively outplayed by Gloucestershire who inherited Lancashire's tendency to block Yorkshire's route to one-day success. Finally, a few years later, the white rose blossomed in a Lords final at the expense of Somerset, courtesy of a century from honorary Yorkshireman, Matthew Elliott. Following the fluctuating fortunes of the once untouchable county of Yorkshire has been a rollercoaster ride, which has only served to render the occasional silverware all the more satisfying. Only Yorkshire, it seems, could proceed from county champions to also-rans in recent years.

BRAGGING RIGHTS

I am gradually becoming disillusioned with the once magical world of football. The amounts of money earned by professionals is obscene, and in a world of poverty and starvation, footballers' wages are an affront to human civilisation – such as it is. Nowadays, footballers 'entertain' with snarling, unpleasant faces, and proceed to surround the referees with their rage and scorn, when the official has dared to pronounce a judgment that is at loggerheads with their plans for world domination. Mis-behaving football players and tantrum-prone managers are horrible role models for impressionable young males.

As for the fans, the support of one football club frequently necessitates a fanatical hatred of rival football clubs. In truth, each major English football club has its own distinctive bragging rights, whether it be Arsenal's 'invincibles' of 2004, Tottenham's outstanding track record in FA Cup finals, Manchester United's treble of 1999, Liverpool's five European Cups, Chelsea's back-to-back Premierships, or even West Ham United's ludicrous claim of having 'won' the 1966 World Cup final. The list could go on to include, amongst others, Aston Villa and Nottingham Forest's European Cup triumphs. It seems that a football supporter clings on to his club's bragging rights to compensate for his or her own personal under-achievement and inadequacies. One only has to observe the reactions of fanatical football supporters to a goal or a result to discover how earth-shatteringly important the occasion is. It is really tragic to think that an individual's state of mind and general well-being is at the mercy of the outcome of a football match. Could there be anything more sad and contemptible?

FOOTBALL UNFOCUSED

Saturday at 12.30 on BBC1, featuring 90 minutes highlights of England's hard-fought 1–1 draw with the Faroes Islands, 2 minutes of Scotland's victory against France, and 90 seconds of Northern Ireland's win against Spain. All brought to you by the 'British' Broadcasting Corporation.

DAILY WEATHER FORECAST FOR THE WIMBLEDON TENNIS TOURNAMENT

First week: Monday – rain, with snowy intervals
Tuesday – rain, with sunny intervals, during which the last remaining British female competitor loses on an outside court at 1pm
Wednesday – rain, with foggy intervals

Thursday – rain, with windy intervals
Friday – rain, with stormy intervals
Saturday – rain, with tornado intervals
Second week: Monday – rain, with hurricane intervals
Tuesday – rain, with typhoon intervals
Wednesday – rain, with hailstone intervals
Thursday – rain, with Sir Cliff Richard intervals
Friday – rain, with dry intervals
Saturday – rain, with wet intervals
Sunday – rain, with tennis intervals

IN THE SUMMERTIME

You can always tell when summer has truly arrived: yet another Brit gets knocked out in the quarter-finals at Wimbledon, the England football team lose another penalty kick shoot-out in a major finals, train drivers on the London Underground take industrial action, and French air traffic controllers go on strike. I cannot wait for the next summer holidays, when my family spend the large majority of our two-week vacation at Heathrow Airport.

ENGLISH-NESS

I think that it was that nice Napoleon Bonaparte who once dismissively described the English/British as a nation of shop-keepers. That flattering portrait can now be replaced by a thoroughly modern interpretation. The English nowadays can be defined as a nation of quarter-finalists. If there were a Third World War, I am supremely confident that England/Britain would be defeated narrowly and gallantly at the quarter-finals stage.

Page 101 refused to give its blessing to this project and so the author and publishers have respectfully left page 101 blank, to respect page 101's wishes. We hope that in the near future page 101 will be persuaded to come on board again. The author and publishers would like to take this opportunity to wish page 101 well, and to apologise to the reader for page 101's boycott of this publication.

THE BRITISH MIDDLE-CLASS

The British middle-class is a herd of selfish, suburban swine. These middle-aged, moralising, disapproving people are intoxicated with selfishness. The tell-tale signs are when they appear on a television news bulletin, letting off considerable steam about such earth-shatteringly important subject as lack of funding for the arts or Britain's association with Europe. Life and death issues such as health service waiting lists, the homeless in their own towns, and famine in the Third World just don't seem to register on their Richter Scales. It is only self-interest that arouses the British middle-class from their smug complacency. When I see a middle-aged, middle-class individual getting agitated about Europe or interest rates, it is clear where their priorities lie – firmly with themselves.

Rising crime and drug abuse in the inner-cities is of no concern for the selfish middle-class. Even the laws of the land were constructed with emphasis on the interests of property and capital, at the expense of personal safety for every individual. Let me explain. An individual who kills someone through drink-driving or who violently assaults someone is likely to receive a lighter sentence than someone who defrauds a fat cat's big business organisation. It is fundamentally clear that money is more valuable than human life if the British judicial system is observed.

The biggest travesty is the National Lottery, a poor man's tax, in which the nation is hoodwinked into spending money on the unattainable goal of a lottery win in order to raise funds for charity. The trouble is that the charity in question tends to be an opera house or a theatre – the staple leisure diets of the middle-class, which is so self-centred that it seemingly can't help itself, and certainly has no intention of helping anyone else. The only redeeming feature of the National Robbery is that it is not screened on ITV. Can you imagine what would happen if it was: 'you will find out what this week's bonus ball is right after this commercial break'.

That nice young man, Johnny Rotten, in his autobiography 'No Irish, No Blacks, No Dogs' (Plexus, 1994) accurately points out that the British middle-class are competitive in all the wrong ways: 'our lawn is better manicured than yours'. What motivates most middle-class people is the need to have a better suite of furniture than their friends and relatives. If I ever become that contemptibly materialistic, I hope that someone will finish me off humanely.

THE BRITISH PRESS

The British public get a raw deal from their newspapers. In the gutter lurk several tabloids (or 'red tops') which don't educate or inform their readers. Their bog standard formula revolves around outrage and screaming headlines, hysteria, panic, sensationalism, trivia, and gossip – some of it malicious. Tabloid journalists are spineless creatures who hide behind their desks and computer screens, and pour merciless vitriol on anyone that they take exception to. To coin a phrase, these peddlers of hate rarely allow the truth to get in the way of a good story. I remain perpetually perplexed as to why so many people sell themselves short by purchasing tabloid rags that offer precious little besides bingo, tits, and sport. Gutter newspapers cater evidently for people with a single-figure I.Q.

At the other end of the journalistic spectrum, we find the pseudo-intellectual newspapers that overwhelm their readers with words and phrases that barely belong in the English language. They word their articles in such an incomprehensible way that only an 'octo-champion' on Countdown could remotely understand. While tabloid newspapers are not shy at dumbing down their apparently dumb readers, broadsheets deliver the kind of gobbledygook jargon which belongs only in the confines of a university lecture theatre. Worse still are the week-end supplement magazines that the broadsheets offer. These supplements contain the biggest amount of filler material that one could possibly imagine, with a plethora of advertisements about exclusive offers and holidays so unaffordable that clearly the readership must consist of mega-rich celebrities and drug dealers. My biggest objection to all British newspapers is that if one removes all the advertisements and all the opinionated columns, we are left with precious little 'news' items.

Finally, in the middle of the market, are the sermonising, self-righteous, holier-than-thou Daily Express and Daily Mail, which have a collective tendency to pander to the xenophobic little Englanders and 'Nimbys'. There is only one thing that British newspapers are good for, and that is for eating fish and chips out of.

BRITAIN'S CONSERVATIVE PARTIES

It is going to be pretty tough deciding which political party to vote for at the next general election, when you consider the following: The Conservative Party are keen to improve the national health service, boost the economy, reduce crime, and revive the education system; while the Labour Conservatives want to improve the national health service, boost the economy, reduce crime, and revive the education system. Alternatively, the Liberal Democrat Conservatives seek to improve the national health service, boost the economy, reduce crime, and guess what, revive the education system. Oh it is going to be an almighty struggle choosing which political party that I will not vote for, when they each have such wonderful plans for the nation. Perhaps I should just pull a party name out of a hat and make the same kind of informed decision that Joe Tabloid and other voters arrive at. If truth be told, the political party that wins most votes is the one with the most convincing liars.

There used to be a predictable cycle in British politics whereby the electorate turfed out the condescending Conservative Party every five years or so in favour of the equally patronising 'we know what's best for you' Labour Conservatives. Nowadays, however, that trend has been replaced by a more tolerant electorate who are prepared to suffer the same patronising Tories in government for about eighteen years before foolishly allowing the condescending Labour Tories to deliver on a fraction of their manifesto promises over a similarly long tenure in office. I am always amused when a political party explains away its general election humiliation by suggesting that they failed to get their message across properly. This is a classic example of denial, when the reality is that the voters were only too painfully aware of their 'misunderstood' message. Is it also not frequently the case that the people who complain about the government are the very same voters who put them in power in the first place? I guess that ultimately the binge drinking, tabloid reading, soap watchers that comprise an unhealthily high proportion of our 'informed' electorate get the government that they so richly deserve.

DOPEY DAVID CAMERON

If that likeable toff David Cameron ever takes up residence at 10 Downing Street, Prime Minister's Question Time could be quite a spectacle, if Mr Cameron's alleged past puffs are to be believed. Imagine the following: "Can the Prime Minister explain to the House, how he intends to respond to the latest crisis in the Middle East"? "Wow man, Middle East crisis, far out".

"Can the Prime Minister kindly inform us how his government intends to cope with the increasing volume of patients waiting in trolleys in hospital corridors for treatment"? "Wow, patients in trolleys in hospital corridors, groovy, man."

GLOBAL WARMING

Any self-respecting fool knows that the environment is important. The conservation of our planet is a matter of concern to most people. Unfortunately, such issues as global warming involve a considerable amount of long-term thinking, but many of us are unavoidably pre-occupied by the here and now. Let me explain. If I am walking home, late at night through the inner city, my thoughts are not with the melting of the polar ice caps, but dominated instead with the question of am I going to get home in one piece. Also, if someone plucks up the courage to visit their GP, suspecting that he or she has found a lump, that person is steeling his or herself for possible bad news, while the greenhouse effect couldn't be further from their mind. Besides, try lecturing to the homeless and starving about the perils of air pollution. Dare I say it, but crime, health, education and poverty will always take priority over the worthy cause of protection of the environment. Global warming is an issue for middle-class people who have too much time on their hands. The rest of us don't have the luxury of merely worrying about the environment.

"EVERYONE HAS A RIGHT TO A PRIVATE PAST"

Well, well, well, so those lovely tabloid correspondents are questioning whether that nice David Cameron is fit for high office on the basis of alleged drug-taking when he was a schoolboy at Eton. How shocking, and here's me thinking that smoking dope was part of the curriculum for every public school. The problem is that if everybody's right to reconstruct their lives after past mis-behaviour is to be undermined by hypocritical, self-righteous journalists, then where do we draw the line? If you punch someone on the face when you are a teenager, does that mean you are not fit to be Home Secretary? If one has a car accident in one's twenties, does that mean one is not suitable to be a minister for transport, or if you have wasted hundreds of pounds buying losing tickets for the National Robbery and Thunderball, does that mean you couldn't be eligible to become a Chancellor of the Exchequer? What if it is 'revealed' that a tabloid hate-peddler failed a school spellings test, would that render he or she invalid for the position of writing for a 'red top'?

We are all flawed individuals, perhaps some more than others. If many brainless, tabloid pen pushers demand that all their parliamentarians be upstanding citizens who neither have taken drugs nor have 'slept around', then the Palace of Westminster would be virtually derelict. There was only one perfect human being, Jesus Christ. Everybody else, both before and since, including David Cameron and other candidates for high office, are a pathetically poor imitation.

LIBERALS

Liberals: don't you just love them madly? They are just a bunch of nice middle-class idealists who like to give everybody the benefit of the doubt. The problem is that these soft touches would gladly and foolishly give lots of benefits to people that the rest of us have lots of doubts about. They believe that every beggar is deserving of our charity and they would like to see every persecuted soul in this world seek asylum in the asylum that is Britain. They feel that murderers and rapists are imprisoned for far too long. They also insist that terror suspects should be released within an hour if they have not kindly confessed. They argue that children should not be chastised too much. They suggest that terrorists are simply misunderstood freedom fighters and that the police are hired thugs who should not arrest anyone unless they are confident that they have at least one hundred witnesses. Liberals stress the need for civil liberties and the liberty of the individual, which is perfectly commendable. However, with all the liberties that liberals want to take, who needs freedom?

THE TRIUMPH OF NEW LABOUR

Margaret Thatcher has reportedly claimed that her greatest legacy is 'New Labour' – a political party that abandoned its socialist roots and re-invented itself in the 1990s as an electable, catch-all party. Whereas the 1972 Watergate burglary was a bungled affair which would impact gravely upon the Nixon administration which sponsored it, the Labour Party's theft of Mrs Thatcher's ideological clothes was a spectacularly successful heist. Gatecrashing the Conservative Party in the mid-1990s and helping themselves to the Tories' wardrobe has enabled the Blairite Labour Party to pose in such right-of-centre clobber as 'tough on crime' and less tolerant of immigration, not to mention a vigorous prosecution of American foreign policy, waging war on anyone remotely associated with international terrorism.

Consequently, Tony Blair stormed to an overwhelming endorsement at the general elections of 1997, 2001, and 2005, while ironically he progressively became less popular within his own political party. The 'rabbit caught in headlights' Conservative Party has therefore been obliged to contest the last two of these elections on a ticket even further to the right of New Labour. The trouble was that the Tories, in their quest to establish clear-blue water between them and New Labour, effectively became a thoroughly unelectable, thinking man's British National Party.

Learning from the debacles of 2001 and 2005, the 'new improved flavour', reconstructed Conservative Party under the leadership of former Etonian and 'man of the people', David Cameron, is almost a throwback to the left-of-centre 'wets' of the Heath administration of the early 1970s. You have to feel some sympathy with the Tories. They have been so hopelessly outflanked by New Labour that they have been denuded of all their traditional clothes that they don't even have a union jack left to wrap around themselves.

Tony Blair may have the appearance of a sanctimonious vicar who misled his country into the Vietnam of Iraq, but to be fair to Tory Blair, he is an accomplished parliamentary performer who has presided over momentous peace initiatives in the formerly insoluble 'Irish question' that tormented the likes of Gladstone, Lloyd George, Heath, Thatcher, and Major.

TONY BLAIR AND WORLD SUMMITS

It must be very awkward and embarrassing for the British Prime Minister when in conversation with the likes of the President of the USA. Imagine the following: "Well Mr President, how's things in the USA these days?" "Yo Blair, we are pioneering new medical research and leading the world in scientific and technological discoveries. So, Blair, how's things in Britain?" "Er, well, we are leading the world in darts and snooker."

Dear oh dear oh dear. This once great sceptred isle of ours with its historic triumphs at Agincourt, Blenheim, Trafalgar, Waterloo, and Rorke's Drift to name but a few. Nowadays, our bragging rights are confined to a couple of blokes rowing fast up and down a river, or cycling very fast round a track. How the once-mighty British Empire has fallen.

UNCLE SAM

Try reciting the 'hallowed' names of Richard Nixon, Ronald Reagan, Bill Clinton, and George 'Dubya' Bush without smiling or breaking out in laughter. It's hard, isn't it? I guess that ultimately the American people get the President that they so richly deserve ... and to think that they regard themselves as a super-power! I don't quite know if it is funny or just plain frightening.

THE SPECIAL RELATIONSHIP

Various politicians and media pundits remind us that Britain has a 'special relationship' with the United States of America. Common sense tells us that it is quite useful to have friends in high places, and they sure don't come much loftier than Uncle Sam. However, is our relationship really 'special'?

Consider the following: The United States was so moved by the mass slaughter of the First World War, that it sat out the conflict for more than three years. Similarly, in the Second World War, while besieged Britain stared at the real possibility of invasion and defeat, the USA took more than two years to come to our aid, and only then because those nice Japanese bombed Pearl Harbor and Adolf Hitler foolishly declared war. However, just when the British congratulated themselves for finding such a helpful ally, the United States proceeded to oppose Britain's invasion of the Suez Canal zone in 1956. Furthermore, Uncle Sam was unwilling to assist Britain in her struggles in the likes of Kenya and Northern Ireland, while again during the Falkland Islands war of 1982, the United States stood with its arms folded. More recently, when Tony Blair exhorted the international community to intervene in Kosovo in 1999, the USA sat on its hands.

By contrast, Britain has allowed her territory to be used as bases for American arms, while Britain has been a little too keen to follow the neo-conservatives' crusade against perceived rogue states and international terrorism. I would dare to suggest that Britain isn't so much Uncle Sam's ally, as his prostitute.

GUNS VERSUS BUTTER

In a country of finite resources, there is the classic economics dilemma of guns versus butter. It is outrageous in the extreme when politicians choose to divert a nation's finances towards armaments (both nuclear and conventional) whilst neglecting to 'feed' its people with improvements in healthcare provision and other such essentials as education and transport infrastructure. How obscene must it be for someone's taxes to be distributed towards weapons of mass destruction – that phrase again. Oh yes, there are weapons of mass destruction to be found in Britain and the United States, though ironically not in 'evil' Iraq.

I cannot for the life of me comprehend the wisdom of investing in useless space exploration and armaments programmes whilst there are homeless on our streets and starving people in the world that our nuclear weapons are supposedly constructed to 'protect'. How would a family feel if the breadwinner spent his or her wages on buying one or two guns for 'self-defence' and not spending money on groceries, a new car, a holiday, new furniture, or home refurbishment? I guess that ultimately, the acquisition of more nuclear weapons is merely an exercise in bragging rights – a recurring theme, in which one country boasts about its strength. Thus, 'a strong defence' is merely a status symbol for a head of state. Have you ever had a conversation where you relate to someone the fact that you went on holiday to Spain for a week only for the other person to reply that "well, we're going on a Caribbean cruise for a month". Similarly, imagine telling someone that you have just bought an apartment in Turkey, only for the other person to respond with "well, we have just bought a big villa in the Bahamas". The arms race is along similar lines in that at a world summit, one head of state claims that his country has 150 nuclear warheads, only for the other one to state " well, my country has 300 nuclear warheads". Perhaps defence spending is not intended for the preservation of national security but is purely for vanity motives.

LIVE 8 – THE SEQUEL

I am pleased to announce the exciting news that there will be another concert extravaganza to raise awareness of poverty in the Third World. At the time of going to press, the assembled entertainers include: Tony Blair on guitar; George Dubya Bush reciting poetry; Gordon Brown doing stand-up comedy; Vladimir Putin performing an organ recital; and a comeback appearance on saxophone from Bill Clinton. These 'artists' are performing in protest against the riches owned by the world's wealthiest people: Elton John, Madonna, Bono, Robbie Williams, Paul McCartney, and Mick Jagger. If these egotistical fat cats donated half their undeserved wealth to the Third World, they would make poverty ancient history.

COMMERCIALISM

I find that there is something distasteful about mega-rich celebrities earning even extra thousands of pounds, endorsing various products in television commercials, where they are encouraging people considerably less well-off than themselves to part with their hard-earned money for a quick fix of a materialistic 'high', thereby going further into debt. There is something lacking in people who throw their scarce resources at unnecessary items of furniture and ornaments to make them feel good about themselves again ... briefly.

THE WORLD'S MOST GENEROUS FAT CATS AND CELEBRITIES

Have you ever read Jesus tell the tale of the poor widow who gave her last remaining coins for charity, a donation which was considerably less than the amount given by the rich man? However, while the rich man donated a tiny fraction of what he owned, the poor widow gave everything that she had. I cannot help but question the lavish praise heaped on all those wonderful stars who are seemingly more charitable than the rest of us, yet in reality give a tiny percentage of their vast wealth to the helpless, while the rest of us mere mortals give much less, yet our donation represents a greater portion of what we possess. For example, do you think that a millionaire's £1,000 donation to famine relief, compared to your gift of £500 means that the tycoon is twice as generous? Oh come on. Think again. If celebrities really wanted to help the poor, they could donate in private, instead of making a big show of their supposed selflessness when they perform for Comic Relief or Live 8, which do no harm for their image and help showcase their talents, thus generating further revenue for their future projects. There is something breathtakingly galling when a rich star appears on screen beseeching the rest of us less fortunate to dip into our pockets and contribute to famine relief. If they are so concerned about the poor and sick, they could eradicate world poverty by selling some of their extra cars, extra houses, and excess clothes. Anyhow, on this page, I have recorded the names of the world's most selfless, generous celebrities and fat cats.

THE POLITICS OF ENVY

Surely if the great David Beckham wanted to re-claim his place in the England football team, he would have returned to the Premiership or at least stayed in Europe and fought his way back into contention for inclusion in the national side. Instead of which, the boy David is off to LA to chase the dollar, showing his true colours of greed, not white or red. I have heard lots of silly people wishing him well, stating that as he is such a nice lad who stays out of trouble, he deserves the obscene amount of money that he will receive from foolishly generous Uncle Sam. There are however many better behaved people than him who earn next to nothing, so let's cut the hero-worship nonsense.

I have heard it suggested by Blokesport day-time presenter, Jon Gaunt, that Beckham and other grossly overpaid entertainers are entitled to their laughably large sums of money. Apparently, anybody who denounces them is just representing the politics of envy. What total tosh, Mr Gaunt. Are starving Africans and/or homeless people just practising the politics of envy? Just how do you silly people out there propose that we find the finances to feed the world and also improve our own healthcare provision? Shall we raise the taxes? Oh no, that is not acceptable. What about increased taxes for the highest earners? Oh perish the thought, that would be an outrage. I can only guess that the government should divert funds from education, defence, or transport infrastructure towards combating poverty and funding our hospitals. You stupid people should realise that governments have to juggle the taxes that we pay into what they deem to be the most worthy causes. Of course, we all know that there is scarcely a politician in human history who has allocated public money to the most deserving causes. After all, we are now informed that the London Olympics is likely to cost about ten billion pounds, four times the original estimate. Far from benefiting the people of Britain, this project for the east end of London is merely an ego exercise for various political figures for whom the 2012 Olympics guarantees them knighthoods and accolades, and like the Millennium Dome before it, the scheme is a burden on the public purse, but hey if the Prime Minister and monarch and mayor of London are sitting in nice seats enjoying the limelight during the Olympic Games, well it will be worth it!

Meanwhile, as people starve in the Third World and fail to receive adequate healthcare even in the western world, we should applaud all the Beckhams, celebrities, and fat cats who line their pockets. Good luck to them, I hear you saying. Oh you foolish people. Will you still accept this monstrous state of affairs when the overworked doctors and underpaid nurses tell you that there is nothing that their hospital can do to save your loved one, because of inadequate resources? Talented stars and sportsmen and women deserve our admiration, but do they then have to go and rob us blind by demanding disgusting amounts of money? Let me guess, Mr Gaunt. My little rant is just another manifestation of the politics of envy. Well, go on then fools and sacrifice yourselves at the altars of those rich peasants that you worship, like the Beckhams. While your loved one lies waiting in a hospital corridor for several hours in order to receive treatment, they are laughing all the way to the bank at our collective stupidity.

CHILDREN IN NEED

When I pay my taxes and National Insurance contributions, I am donating to children in need – in theory. In reality however, the government chooses to divert my generous funds to armaments to slaughter other countries' children in need. If I had a pound for every time the government wasted taxpayers' money, I could take an early retirement. The tragedy is that if our taxes were not squandered, but invested in healthcare, education, and eradicating poverty, there would be no need for celebrities and lesser egos humiliating themselves each November for children in need.

BEGGARS

One of the great developments of the enlargement of the European Union is that east Europeans now have the life-changing career opportunity to sell copies of the Big Issue on the streets of Britain. A lot of people are uncomfortable, not to say irritated, by the beggars and charity collectors on our streets. To the dismay of liberals, my advice is not to give to beggars, because it only encourages them. We do have a system of social security for people short of money and adequate housing. Those who are begging for money should take advantage of this system. Those who refuse to do so, I beg to venture, are not British citizens.

On a lighter note, I am pleased to report that I have found the solution to how to cope with beggars: When I am confronted with one such unfortunate soul, I simply pull out of my pocket a copy of my latest bank statement and show it to the beggar who then apologises and offers me his last five pence.

EAST EUROPEANS IN BELFAST

I recently found myself asking why so many people were migrating from eastern Europe to sunny Belfast, when it suddenly struck me that they wanted to find somewhere grim that would remind them of a communist country. Oh come on, Belfast people, don't be so bloody touchy.

DAVINA McCALL: THE MOVIE

Starring Davina McCall as the megalomaniac presenter in the big boots with an inflated sense of self-importance. (Film length: 187 minutes), sponsored by the *Carphone Warehouse.*

JOIN THE ARMED FORCES

Wear a pretty uniform. See the world. Fight and die in a foreign country, far from family and friends, for a cause you don't believe in and for a government you don't support. Or alternatively, get captured and then suffer such torture as being forced to play table tennis. Then sell your story and your soul to a trashy tabloid. Don't delay; visit your nearest recruiting officer today.

GAMBLING

There is a myth that book-makers cannot be beaten. In fact, I have been helpfully told that you will rarely (if ever) see a bookie on a bike – more likely in a BMW or Mercedes. However, my mixed fortunes as a gambler have demonstrated that you can change your life for better or for worse by having a hopeful punt. I came close to cracking the code to the safe, but ultimately I painfully discovered that gambling is one step forward, two steps back. I used to win big, but lose very big too. I was not interested in fun bets of a few pounds. I failed to see the thrill in having a silly little bet on a horse in a twenty-horse race, whose chances of winning, despite its proven track record, was basically one in twenty. The best gambles, in my semi-humble opinion, ought to be based on studying the mathematical probability of various outcomes, whilst ignoring the obvious. After all, if the obvious certainties really were certainties, then book-makers would never win, which isn't exactly the case. I concentrated on singles bets where I backed one football team to beat another or one horse to finish ahead of another. In these instances, there are two possible outcomes for the latter bet and three different potential outcomes for the former scenario. Anybody who invests in accumulators is badly mistaken. Such bets were deliberately created by book-makers in the safe knowledge that the chances of winning are remote. Those football punters who for example back a mere four teams to win their respective matches should understand that the mathematical probability of this, irrespective of so-called form, is 1 in 81, although you won't find the clever book-makers paying out £81 if you invest £1. Even this smart alec discovered that backing one cricket or rugby team to beat another is not as simple as it seems. I mean, if it were a straight-forward path to riches, do you think that I would feel the need to write this book?

I could repeat the old cliché that my only gambling problem was losing, but the major trouble that I have with gambling is that one tends to end up adopting a gambling psyche in other areas of one's life. Gambling on football, greyhounds, and horses is one thing, but taking gambles in the traffic lane on the motorway, or gambling with other people's lives is far more serious.

THIEVES LIKE US

Every time that I step into a supermarket, an announcement immediately goes out in the store's intercom: "could all security personnel return to their close circuit television screens at once". I can no longer go shop-lifting, without fear of being watched and intimidated. What is this society coming to? Worst of all, supermarkets are just a social club where folks meet one another and exchange progress reports on their lengthy wait for a hip replacement operation. Then you get those couples who wish to share their dietary habits with an unwilling audience: "love, don't get those baked beans again; you know they don't agree with me."

VETTING

There is so much vetting in modern society that it is becoming quite ridiculous. Let me quote an example, children. I recently browsed through job vacancies in a newspaper whereupon one particular advertisement caught my eye. It announced: 'Bank Job; driver required.' I decided to apply, confident of my ability to drive many people to distraction, which ought to be sufficient credentials for a driving vacancy. Well, imagine my surprise when it transpired that the employers were not NatWest or Barclays, but a south London 'firm' who needed someone to drive their getaway car at the successful conclusion of their projected 'bank job'.

What astounded me was their application form, yes application form, which asked amongst other things, if I had a criminal record. What?! I was staggered that a firm intent on robbing a bank wanted to know if I had any convictions. Perhaps any past transgressions would be advantageous, I did not know. To add insult to injury, and I was feeling mentally very injured, I was asked at my subsequent interview if I possessed a clean driving licence. Extraordinary. I was applying to drive a getaway car, and this was the extent of their scrutiny. I tell you, ladies and gentlemen, there is now too much vetting in our beloved world.

CAPITAL PUNISHMENT

When we hear that a child has been mauled to death by a dangerous dog, we are informed that the animal was subsequently 'destroyed'. If truth be told, the owners of dangerous dogs are the real animals. However, in the contentious debate over the death penalty, should dangerous people not be 'destroyed' too? I would personally advocate capital punishment for multiple murderers, who either kill on more than one occasion or who murder more than one person. Such criminals, like bombers, have no regard for human life, and are distinguishable from those people who kill once only – perhaps in revenge against an abuser. For Christians, capital punishment is a divisive issue. On the one hand, surely God expects us to govern ourselves and apply law in accordance with his guidance and teachings. On the other hand, God has stated to those of us on the receiving end of injustice, that 'vengeance is mine; I will re-pay'.

CRIME

First we had crimes of passion and now we have hate crimes. What will be next? I have a terrifying vision of the future that we will have crimes of indifference. Your neighbour could become the most feared person in your life, far more frightening than Al-Queda. Killing someone out of motives of 'love' or hate is one thing, but committing crimes purely out of apathy or boredom is a lot more scary.

Do you know that the safest, most law-abiding citizens in our society are lazy layabouts? Such persons are so lacking in motivation that they cannot be bothered – doing anything. Almost all crimes require motives, but individuals without motivation are unlikely to break the law. Until they drag themselves out of bed and away from daytime television, such lazy layabouts are the most upstanding citizens in our country.

CRIME DOES PAY

Isn't it appalling to find hard-working people living on top of each other in high rise blocks and/or in streets of unremarkable terraced houses while fat cats and other criminals live in the detached houses of suburbia. Let me dispel any illusions. For every ten grand houses on the edge of town, you will find at least one occupant who doesn't make an honest living. Nobody ever got rich from working 9 to 5, Monday to Friday. However, let's not pick on the poor, defenceless drug dealers and other entrepreneurs in their Chelsea tractors and Spanish villas. The biggest crooks in our society are the Premiership footballers, golfers, snooker players, tennis stars, pop stars, and so-called television entertainers who earn (what a ridiculous word) obscene amounts of money. That we all allow the massive disparity in wages between the haves and the have nots to persist is the biggest crime of all. To add insult to injury, celebrities are afforded greater legal protection, via the best solicitors and barristers that money can buy, in contrast to us lesser mortals. Only in America, after all, can a 'star' get away with murder or even child abuse. Not only does crime pay, but it reaps handsome dividends.

POLICE AND THIEVES

There are a lot of unsolved crimes in our country, and the reason that villains get off the hook, given license to terrorise the streets, is because not only do smarty pants solicitors pick holes in cases for the prosecution of suspected criminals, but because the public are unable and/or unwilling to furnish the police with sufficient evidence to secure an arrest and conviction. Consider the following scenario:

Joe Public: Hello, I would like to report a burglary that took place in my house.
Police Officer: What was stolen, sir?
Joe Public: A television.
Police Officer: Oh dear. I don't suppose that you saw the burglar, did you?
Joe Public: Oh yes.
Police Officer: Good, well give me a description then.
Joe Public: He had two legs.
Police Officer: Two legs. Are you quite sure?
Joe Public: Oh yes.
Police Officer: Anything else that springs to mind?
Joe Public: If I'm not very much mistaken, he had two arms as well.
Police Officer: Remarkable. Definitely two arms?
Joe Public: Well ... I am at least 90% certain.
Police Officer: Can you recall anything else, sir?

Joe Public: I seem to remember he had one ear on one side of his head and another ear on the other side.

Police Officer: Okay. Were there any other distinguishing features?

Joe Public: The burglar was wearing some clothes.

Police Officer: Any particular colour?

Joe Public: Oh all sorts of different colours.

Police Officer: What about his skin colour? Was he black or white?

Joe Public: Oh yes, absolutely.

Police Officer: Absolutely what?

Joe Public: He was definitely either black or white.

Police Officer: Is there anything else that you can tell us which might help our enquiries?

Joe Public: Come to think of it, there is. It's all coming back to me now. He had two eyes, two hands, and two feet. Oh yes, and he was at least five foot tall, possibly as big as six foot seven. Do you think that you will catch him?

Police Officer: Well sir, according to your description, we will be conducting a manhunt in search of a man, possibly either black or white in complexion, between five foot and six foot seven in height, who has two legs, two arms, two eyes, two hands, two feet, with one ear on either side of his head, and who was wearing clothes of different colours.

DEADLINE

The latest Hollywood blockbuster bullshit, about Joe Maverick's lone struggle to overcome the forces of evil and save the planet from destruction, with only 24 hours left to do so. Featuring the Pentagon, National Security, the President and the White House, Whitehall, the Prime Minister, the CIA, the FBI, MI5, MI6, Interpol, the PLO, James Bond, Blofeld, and the KGB. A must-see for all silly little men who are turned on by such nonsense.

OUR PERVERSE SOCIETY

No, I am not going to pour scorn on the breath-taking hypocrisy of tabloid newspapers that scream outrage at the activities of a paedophile on one page while sexily portraying a teen sensation on the facing page. Instead, I am more concerned at the growing trend in the summer of men wearing shorts, while women wear trousers. Can there be anything more perverse than men showing off their hairy legs, and women hiding their (hairy) legs? Worst of all, a heatwave gives license to all sorts of less than attractive people to go out shopping, scantily clad. Yuk! If that is not bad enough, we have to endure the sight of seventy-somethings wearing shorts, sandals, and grey socks. I look at these coffin dodgers, and I wonder to myself about how we ever managed to win two world wars. (Disclaimer: the United States and France helped a bit too.) I then realise the truth: that granddad, rest his soul, landed on the beaches at Anzio or Normandy in his shorts, sandals, and grey socks. The Germans took one look at him, dropped their guns, and quite understandably made a run for it.

WHAT NOT TO WEAR

I would dearly like to pass myself off as a fashion expert, but that would be stretching credibility just a tad, I fear. Nevertheless, I remain horrified to find young men still sporting dreadful cheque shirts, as modelled by Jack Sugden of *Emmerdale*. These fashion accessories belong on the kitchen table, lying spread-eagled underneath the plates and assembled crockery. Even more disturbing than this glorified table-cloth is the tendency for a lot of silly little twenty-something men to wear tee-shirts in mid-winter. What's that all about? Oh yes, I know, it is a pathetic display of supposed macho masculinity. Sorry chaps, but it is just an exhibition of plain stupidity. When I see a silly little girl, arm in arm with a cheque-shirted (or in winter with a tee-shirted) young man, I think to myself, 'there but for the grace of God go I'.

Anyhow, here follows a selection of my fashion tips on what not to wear, ladies and gentlemen:

A balaclava in a building society branch
Your birthday suit at a funeral
Wellington boots at a disco (well, at least they didn't work for me)
A police uniform in prison
A track-suit at an interview for a civil service job
Pyjamas at work
A swastika in a synagogue
A turban at a BNP meeting
An orange sash at Parkhead
A Celtic football jersey in an Orange hall
An Arsenal scarf at White Hart Lane
A duffel coat in the desert
Sunglasses in the dark
A swimsuit at the North Pole
Clothes in a nudist colony
A hooded coat in a jewellery shop
Tee-shirts in the winter
Cheque shirts during any season or occasion

Jeans on a date. Oh come on folks. Jeans are for the building site or for sitting in the house or the pub.

Trousers on a woman. Come on ladies, if I wanted to date someone wearing trousers, I would find myself a man.

ANONYMITY BIG BROTHER

For the first time ever, I watched the opening night of D-List Celebrity Big Brother. It was laughable watching these famous people greet each other for the first time. In fact, they were so well-known that nobody seemed to know each other. Surely it would have been helpful if each 'contestant' had adorned a large name tag, with their occupation included. I bet some of them suspected that one of their group was just another non-celebrity from the great unwashed, planted in their midst like Chantelle, d'you know what I mean? Oh my God.

I watched the first night with mixed feelings after my application to appear on Anonymity Big Brother had been rejected. Unfortunately, I was informed that I was far too recognisable for the show. What they required instead were famously unknown 'stars'. I must confess that I wish Celebrity Big Brother was on every month, so that we can see more of our super-heroes expose the myth that entertainers and stars are better human beings than the rest of us. It's reassuring to know that our famous idols are as rude, foul-mouthed, and obnoxious as the rest of us. How fitting it was that the top three in the last outing of Anonymity Big Brother were all foreigners. We only have ourselves to blame for nurturing a nation of white trash. I don't believe that Jade Goody was racist, but she was certainly a bully. Can you imagine being stuck in a lift with her? A fate worse than death, methinks. To be honest, the remark 'Shilpa Poppadum' was merely a throwback to the days when the politically correct bigots didn't censor our screens and we were all able to watch the light-hearted banter of the likes of 'Mind Your Language', 'Love Thy Neighbour', 'It Aint Half Hot Mum', and 'In Sickness And In Health'. Such programmes would infuriate the PC plonkers who decide what constitutes public good taste nowadays.

Anyhow, dear old Donny Whatsitsname had the right approach to Pondlife Big Brother: he came , made a splash, and then left before he might make an even bigger fool of himself. Punk rockers are a lot more intelligent than they are given credit for.

CELEBRITY SQUARES

I just loathe those dreadful 'chat shows' where two big egos collide in an exercise of mutual back-slapping and produce a completely contrived conversation. It is frequently the case that the very special guest, so-called, has sacrificed fifteen minutes of his or her precious time to relentlessly plug his or her new film, record or book. It is a real shame that bookshops are overflowing with books by celebrities, who are not writers by profession while other genuine scribes struggle to find a place on the shelf. Most celebrity books are simply an unashamed attempt to cash in on fleeting popularity. Meanwhile, in a television interview, if the host dares to ask the star guest how he or she is coping with their drug addiction problem, the viewer is informed "oh you can find the answer to my struggles with drugs in Chapter Seven of my new autobiography, which will be available in the shops this forthcoming Monday for only £16.99". More often than not however, the guest normally has to work hard to get a word in about his or her new project because it is the host who jealously preserves his or her status as the real star of the show. If one ever observes the likes of Paul O'Grady, Jonathon Woss, and Frank Skinner, it is apparent that the host is ever so keen to dominate the so-called conversation, which they punctuate at regular intervals with their bog standard clever-dick remarks. Quite clearly they perceive the guest's role as that of an ornament designed to decorate their humour.

I nevertheless reserve special contempt for Charlotte Church who has appallingly re-invented herself as a loud-mouthed, attention seeker, who (choosing my words carefully) could do a good impersonation of a Welsh whore. Did you ever see anything quite as ridiculous as Miss Church hosting the esteemed 'Have I Got News For You'? It's enough to drive Angus Deayton to drugs. The trouble I have with Miss Church is that city centre streets, taxis, and buses are plagued by Charlotte Church clones on Friday and Saturday nights. Girl power, far from liberating young women, has empowered them with a lippy attitude that does no favours to the female species. No, I am not some Mr Cholmondly-Warner who believes that women should be seen and not heard, but hey ladies let's try and behave yourselves. Don't allow the Charlotte Churches to drag you down towards the excessive mis-behaviour of many young males.

Most celebrities are merely supremely untalented, one trick ponies and extremely fortunate. Gordon Ramsey's reputation is built on his over-indulgence in foul-mouthed outbursts, but my next door neighbour knows how to swear a lot, and yet he doesn't get a television show out of it. Similarly, my granny could cook better than the ubiquitous Jamie Oliver, but she doesn't get a cookery programme. Furthermore, don't get me started on that ghastly 'Friday Night Project', that Tiswas for twenty-somethings, that Multi-Coloured Swap Shop for adults in denial about their age. Every week they predictably cheer and go hooray at the guest presenter. I bet that even if Colonel Gaddafi or Osama Bin Laden was the guest presenter, the silly audience would still cheer 'hooray'. Oh what sad, silly people. As for 'Baddiel And Skinner Unplanned', don't make me laugh. I was 'unplanned', but my parents didn't get a television show out of it.

CHANNEL FOUR'S CHRISTMAS DAY BROADCASTING SCHEDULE

There is a clique of celebrities who swamp the schedules on Channel Four. Even in commercial breaks one finds the Channel Four mafia of Alan Carr, Jimmy Carr, Russell Brand (Jo Brand's secret love child), Gordon Ramsey, and Jamie Oliver giving their vox populi on topics such as my biggest indulgence or greatest regret. Any would–be television entertainer has their work cut out to kick the Channel Four mafia into touch. Anyhow, I have revealed a sneak preview of Channel Four's Christmas Day schedule for this year:

4.15–5.00: Countdown with Carol Vorderman (and Jimmy Carr in dictionary corner)
5.00–7.00: Gordon Ramsey's Kitchen Nightmares
7.00–9.00: How To Open Your Christmas Presents, presented by Alan Carr
9.00–11.00: Preparing The Christmas Dinner, with Jamie Oliver (who else)

11.00–13.00: A Documentary On The Life Of Gordon Ramsey
13.00–15.00: Jo Brand's Favourite Christmas Memories
15.00–15.30: The Queen's Christmas Message, translated by Jamie Oliver
15.30–16.15: Countdown with Carol Vorderman (with Graham Norton in dictionary corner)
16.15–17.00: Celebrity Deal Or No Deal (guests Jamie Oliver and Jimmy Carr)
17.00–18.00: The Paul O'Grady Show, with very special guest Russell Bland
18.00–19.00: What To Do With Your Turkey Leftovers, presented by Gordon Ramsey
19.00–20.00: Channel Four News, presented by Jimmy Carr
20.00–22.00: School Dinners, with Jamie Oliver, and special guest Gordon Ramsey
22.00–Midnight: Late Night Discussion On Christmas, chaired by Russell Bland

SOAPS

Contrary to popular myth, I am familiar with soaps. What baffles me about television soaps is that nobody ever seems to be sitting in their living room, watching another soap. For example, I have yet to see Vera Duckworth say to Jack that she isn't going to the Rovers Return tonight, because she wants to stay in and watch an episode of *Eastenders*. Similarly, I have never once heard that pleasant, happy-go-lucky Pauline Fowler in the last twenty years pay tribute to the merits of the *Emmerdale* scriptwriters. I mean, how many of you have ever witnessed one of the characters in *Neighbours* having a look at *Home And Away*? I concede that *Coronation Street* and *Eastenders* do have their moments, but my favourite soap is unquestionably Cussons' Imperial Leather. As for Aussie soaps and British soaps, I wash my hands of them.

TEARS OF A CLOWN

Many people, predominantly of an older generation, can testify to the big contribution that Tony Hancock, Spike Milligan, and Peter Sellers made to providing light relief in their lives. It is hugely ironic that these three gifted 'funny men' (and a few others besides) had the knack of making other people laugh, yet these individuals were at times thoroughly unpleasant and hard to live with. It is a massive burden for a comedian when everyone expects he or she to be full of the joys of spring 24/7. Hancock was so prone to depression that he took his own life in Australia in 1968, whilst Milligan was no stranger to a breakdown or two. Sellers, if biographer Roger Lewis is to be believed, had more than his share of demons which gravely impacted upon his loved ones and friends. It is the mother of all paradoxes that these three entertainers were exceptionally funny and yet thoroughly miserable. The word schizophrenia springs to one of my two minds.

PARIS

What is it with celebrities and Paris? It is amazing the number of famous personages who go to Paris and die there. To name but a few, we have had Oscar Wilde (aka Sebastian Melmoth), Jim Morrison (the lizard king, who could do anything), the Shah of Iran, Princess Diana and Dodi-el-Fayad, and most recently Yasser Arafat. Paris must be one enormous graveyard. When I become famous (any day soon) I will avoid gay Paris like the plague. Actually, I got momentarily excited the other day when my next-door neighbour said he was going on holiday to France. Regrettably, he said he was planning to stay in Bordeaux, although I did encourage him to pay a visit to Paris.

GREAT BRITAIN

Almost one million men in the First World War, and nearly half a million men in the Second World War gave their lives so that this country could be free: free to produce and listen to dreadful pop music; free to binge drink; free to run riot at football matches and in town centres on Friday and Saturday nights; free to produce and watch tacky drivel on television; free to bully minorities and hate foreigners; free to be educated by tabloid newspapers. Isn't it so comforting to know that the sacrifices of all those brave young souls was not in vain? Isn't Britain just Great?

MBEs

How absurd that various esteemed individuals of our country are designated as members or officers of an empire that has long since vanished. Knighthoods, like most awards, are frequently conferred on the wrong people. I would venture to say that for every outstanding 'star' who is awarded an MBE, there are at least ten doctors, nurses, or members of the emergency services considerably more deserving of this daft accolade. Consider some of those whose wonderful efforts have merited a gong. Rod Stewart? Don't make me chuckle. Why reward this wealthy, foul-mouthed old tart? As for the England cricket team, having had their collective bottoms spanked in the southern hemisphere by Australia and Pakistan in recent winters, Freddie and the dreamers should 'do a John Lennon' and hand their MBEs back. Ultimately, in the absence of the British Empire, I can only assume that the awards are for Monstrously Big Egos, Outrageously Big Egos, and Completely Big Egos.

GOD SAVE THE QUEEN

Why are the British so infatuated with the institution of monarchy? There is something logic-defyingly irrational about supporting a family who live in luxury in central London, a paltry few hundred yards from homeless people, whose accommodation isn't palatial, but consists either of a sleeping bag or a cardboard box, or maybe both if they are particularly well off. No doubt you silly royal lovers will suggest that the poor deserve everything that is coming to them, while the royal family deserve every last million pounds, Rolls Royce, and palace that they possess.

Monarchists, amongst other things, like to boost their flimsy arguments with gibberish about how our monarchy renders Britain the envy of the world. Wake up people and stop taking leave of your senses. The history of the British monarchy is far from noble or glorious. Richard The Lionheart, Edward IV, James I, and William III were homosexuals, allegedly, while Queen Anne is rumoured to have had a sexual relationship with Sarah Churchill. George III apparently was of such sound mind that he addressed an oak tree one day in the mistaken belief that he was in conversation with the King of Prussia. It didn't stop him from ruling for a staggering sixty years during which time his kingdom was humiliated by the loss of the American colonies. Edward VIII's biggest failing wasn't that he married a divorcee in preference to remaining as king, but that he and his American missus deemed that nice, broad-minded democrat Adolf Hitler worthy of a visit, thereby handing the evil Nazis many propaganda bonus points. Edward VII and King Charles II were not exactly one-woman men, so folks, as you can see, the royal family has scarcely ever been paragons of family values and virtue. I haven't even mentioned the kings and queens who were merely bloodthirsty, sadistic, bigots and racists. Only our three most recent monarchs deserve exemption from the hall of shame.

Still, apparently we must cling on to the monarchy for dear life. Why? Well, let's consider the benefits of having a monarchy then, in great detail:

1. Tourism.
2. Also, tourism.
3. They benefit tourism.
4. The Royal Family boosts tourism.
5. The monarchy helps our tourism.
6. They're good for tourism.
7. Not forgetting tourism.
8. Tourism too.
9. The royals make a big contribution to tourism.
10. Did I mention tourism?

Meanwhile, here is a list of useful things those lovely, overworked and underpaid royals should do:

1. Abdicate en masse.
2. Get a proper job and earn a living, like the rest of us.
3. Resign en masse.
4. Retire en masse.

Of course Queen Elizabeth I is a woman who carries herself with great dignity amidst the soap opera that is the Windsors, but it is high time the British infant emerged from its womb, and cut off the umbilical cord of monarchy to take its proper place in a brave new world. As for that ghastly national anthem, surely you dyed in the wool monarchists concede that 'Jerusalem' would be a more preferable anthem. Personally, I think that 'God Save The Queen' should be replaced by the more appropriate 'God Help Us'.

THE MYTH OF THE SEX PISTOLS

Many students and middle-class, middle-aged teenagers still lavish praise on the apparent wonder that was 'Never Mind The Bollocks'. I am a bit astonished to find this mediocre record occupying lofty positions in all-time, best-ever albums lists. As a museum piece of a remarkable chapter in modern British social history, 'Never Mind The Bollocks' is worthy of investment. However, to suggest that this cycle of cacophonous tunes merits repeated listening is stretching the imagination a bit. True, Paul Cook, Steve Jones, and Glen Matlock were better musicians than perhaps they have been credited with.

However, the undoubted 'star' of those loveable Pistols was Johnny Rotten, who like Shaun Ryder after him, was more of a 'vocalist' than a singer, each possessing the musical talent of a block of wood. Nevertheless, Rotten was and still is an amusing, highly intelligent, and compelling free-thinker who has more brain cells than most tabloid journalists who have lampooned him, put together. It was Rotten's victorious pursuit of financial justice at the hands of the real villain, Malcolm McLaren, that woke people, not least Cook and Jones, up to the fact that the apparent street urchin John Lydon was not to be under-estimated. Sorry to explode the myths of the Sex Pistols, but Rotten's best musical offerings have surfaced intermittently in the guise of Public Image Limited, courtesy of gems such as 'Flowers Of Romance', 'Rise', and the outstanding 'Warrior'. Ironically, it was the post-Rotten 'The Great Rock'n'Roll Swindle' soundtrack which yielded perhaps the best punk rock tunes, namely the title track as well as Sid Vicious's 'interpretation' of Eddie Cochran's 'Somethin' Else', and 'C'mon Everybody', three tracks that epitomise what rock and roll should sound like. Only 'Clash City Rockers' surpasses these punk highlights. Those silly people, young and older ones who should know better, who think that 'Never Mind The Bollocks' is a great record, to coin a Rotten phrase,

just
didn't
get
it.

THE MYTH OF SERGEANT PEPPER'S LONELY HEARTS CLUB BAND

I remain amazed that so many self-appointed expert commentators, not to mention our Mums and Dads, regard Sergeant Pepper (1967) as the greatest album of all time. For a start, it is not even The Beatles' best 33 $^1/_3$. Some people prefer its predecessors, Rubber Soul (1965) and Revolver (1966), but this young man believes that the so-called White Album (1968) and Abbey Road (1969) are the Fab Four's best album offerings. Furthermore, Pepper was not even the best album to emerge from EMI's Abbey Road recording studios in 1967. That distinction belongs with Pink Floyd's debut long-player 'The Piper At The Gates Of Dawn'.

Furthermore, as an exercise in psychedelia, Sergeant Pepper is hardly choc full of mind-expanding material. Commentators will predictably point to Lucy In The Sky With Diamonds, but Paul McCartney's products such as Lovely Rita, Getting Better, and When I'm Sixty-Four are about as 'far out, man' as a Max Bygraves album.

Of course the album's cover and montage of assorted heroes and anti-heroes merit much praise, but as an exercise in hype and myth, Pepper is the ultimate let-down. True, there are musical highlights, such as George Harrison's 'Within You, Without You', which sounded absolutely nothing like anything that had been inserted on a pop album before. Similarly, 'A Day In The Life' is an equally unique track that sounds like nothing recorded before or in four decades since. The greatest tragedy of Sergeant Pepper is that the outstanding double A-side, Strawberry Fields Forever and Penny Lane, were omitted from the album. Pepper is yet another good record from an excellent group of musicians, nothing more, nothing less.

SMILE: THE GREATEST ALBUM THAT NEVER WAS

In 1964 Brian Wilson, Beach Boys' singer and songwriter, had a breakdown which resulted in him advising the rest of the group that they should find a replacement for their touring commitments, while Brian would devote his energies to composing new material and working in the recording studio. Initially Glen Campbell was drafted in, before the likeable Bruce Johnston was appointed as Wilson's touring substitute.

America's answer to the Fab Four entertained audiences worldwide with their simple pop formula based around pretty girls, cars, and surfing (an activity that was actually foreign to them, except drummer Dennis Wilson). Meanwhile, the supremely talented Brian now found the time to stretch the group's creativity as he sought to surpass The Beatles and the sounds of ace producer Phil Spector. First of all, in response to hearing the ground-breaking album 'Rubber Soul'(1965), Wilson resolved to reply with an artistic statement of his own. Wilson's riposte was the incomparably beautiful 'Pet Sounds'(1966), a record that blended pop harmonies with a wide range of instruments performed by the best session musicians that Brian could assemble. The emotions of hope and despair that represented 'Pet Sounds' did not meet with unanimous approval in the American album charts, but critical acclaim on both sides of the Atlantic persuaded Wilson to launch into an even loftier project which, it was anticipated, would blow away all competitors, Beatles included.

Recruiting a young man called Van Dyke Parks to provide the lyrics, Wilson feverishly assembled ideas and songs for his next album which had the working title of 'Dumb Angel', before evolving into 'Smile'. The trouble was that as Wilson was scaling his artistic peak, the substances that had stimulated his creativity on 'Pet Sounds' were now undermining his progress. Hashish and LSD were beginning to wreck havoc in the mind of an already emotionally fragile individual. Wilson, traumatised by a bullying father, and struggling to sell his new ideas to the rest of the Beach Boys became progressively unbalanced. Consequently, Brian conceived a plethora of plans for 'Smile', only to abandon them soon after, including flirtations with health food, the desire to produce an album of sound effects, and also a record devoted to humour. Even Van Dyke Parks, author of 'far out' lyrics, was embarrassed by Wilson's unhinged, 'far out' behaviour.

Then, as Capitol Records and the rest of the pop world rubbed their hands at the imminent release of 'Smile', Brian pulled the plug on the album, and its release was scrapped as Wilson mistakenly feared that the issue of 'Sergeant Pepper's Lonely Hearts Club Band' was too good to compete against. What a tragedy that Wilson's 'teenage symphony to God' was shelved, surfacing in part in the anaemic 'Smiley Smile'. Tracks such as 'Good Vibrations', 'Heroes And Villains', and the formidable harmonies of 'Surf's Up' would have kicked the hyped Pepper into touch. After losing his nerve, not to mention his marbles, Wilson and his group absented themselves from the Monterey pop festival, and while The Beach Boys soldiered on with varying degrees of success, Brian retreated to his bedroom for the best part of ten years, even installing a refrigerator in his bedroom so that he would not have to venture far for a snack.

By the mid-1970s, Wilson was a beached whale in self-imposed exile who had missed the bus. Yet, remarkably, three decades later Brian is back on stage basking in the glory of the long overdue release of 'Smile'. If eccentricity and genius are two sides of the same coin, then Wilson, ace composer and producer, possesses that penny. What summed up the erratic behaviour of Brian during the 'Smile' sessions was his method acting approach to the recording of the 'Fire' segment of a suite entitled 'The Elements'. Wilson instructed the classical-trained musicians to adorn toy replicas of fireman's hats during the recording of 'Fire'. However, when Brian subsequently discovered that a nearby building had burned down simultaneous to this extraordinary recording session, Wilson decreed that the 'vibes' were ominously bad, and 'Fire' joined other 'Smile' tapes in a vault ,out of harm's way. My favourite observation of Brian Wilson, wayward genius, emanates from the late Derek Taylor, publicist for The Beatles and The Beach Boys, who explained that being in the company of Brian was akin to the Mad Hatter's Tea Party: 'have some tea; there isn't any'. (The Dark Stuff, by Nick Kent, Penguin, 1994)

TACKY TRASH

Join Graham Norton (who else) on Saturday nights as the BBC auditions many hopefuls in the search for the new Shane MacGowan. Relentlessly plugged for several weeks, after every BBC programme.

LIKE A ROLLING STONE: THE MYTH OF BRIAN JONES

Long before punk rock, heavy metal, grunge, or gangsta rap set about creating sizeable generation gaps, there existed a notorious quintet called The Rolling Stones. Marketed as the antithesis of the four loveable Moptops from Liverpool, the 'Strolling Ruins' were the bad boys of popular music. Their manager, Andrew Loog Oldham, himself no shrinking violet, asked 'would you let your daughter marry a Rolling Stone?' To the dismay of many disapproving parents, many a young woman would have accepted the considerable challenge.

Before the Stones became Keef's group in all but name, the most challenging, attractive, and charismatic stone was Brian Jones. Gifted with blond good looks, not to mention the versatility to tackle a range of musical instruments, Jones was the hustler who kick-started the industry that became known as The Rolling Stones. However, by the mid-sixties, Jones had allowed himself to be out-flanked by the Jagger and Richards songwriting axis, and succumbing to the trappings of stardom, Jones overdosed on sex, drink, and drugs, becoming one of the sixties most infamous party animals. The trouble was that as Mick and Keith's partnership sustained The Rolling Stones, Jones became marginalised, as well as victimised by two drug busts, one of which had 'fit-up' written all over it. Consequently, Jones started sliding into a personal oblivion. His appearance at the recording studios was neither guaranteed nor productive, if indeed he was sober enough to make the effort.

By June 1969, the inevitable happened. Brian Jones was deemed surplus to requirements by a group that was keen to tour the United States for the first time in three years, and so Mick Taylor was drafted in as a replacement. Jones's divorce from the group that he had formed was a remarkably civil affair, with the standard 'musical differences' cited as the explanation for the separation. Jones was now left to his own devices at his new country residence of Cotchford Farm in Sussex, the former home of A.A Milne, author of 'Winnie The Pooh'. No sooner were The Rolling Stones preparing for their new future than their old comrade and former guitarist was found floating in his pool in the early hours of the 3rd of July. For many observers of Jones, his premature death at the age of 27 was a natural culmination of his self-destruct lifestyle. Small wonder then that a coroner's inquest pronounced 'death by misadventure'.

However, there has always been something fishy about the drowning of Brian Jones, a strong swimmer. For about 35 years, all manner of suggestions and conspiracy theories have been floated (no pun intended). Perhaps Jones was bumped off on the instructions of his former group, or maybe that nice Keith Richards was lurking behind the bushes waiting to apply the dirty deed. It now appears likely, if a recent television documentary is to be believed, that Brian Jones was murdered by Frank Thorogood, who allegedly made a death-bed confession in recent years. Thorogood had been working at Jones's house, and under the influence of alcohol, a difference of opinion in the swimming pool appears to have had fatal consequences. Jones could be both charming and obnoxious, so there was no shortage of enemies. The truth may never be known, but 'death by misadventure' was a fitting verdict for someone who lived his life by misadventure. Whatever became of The Rolling Stones?

ALTAMONT: THE DEATH OF THE SIXTIES

The latter half of the 1960s was a time of massive cultural and social upheaval on both sides of the Atlantic Ocean. While war raged in Vietnam and the threat of a nuclear holocaust lurked in the background, a youth revolution occurred. Embracing the 'hip' ideals of love and peace, flower power was the young generation's response to the global Cold War. Pop festivals such as Monterey, California in June 1967 and Woodstock, New York in August 1969 witnessed an outpouring of optimism among the hippies that their vision of 'make love, not war' would usurp the cynicism of the older generation.

However, it was not that simple. Despite the best of intentions, the flower power revolution paved the way for riots on the streets of Paris and Belfast in 1968 and 1969 as well as violent anti-war protests in London and in the United States. Furthermore, the 'turn on, tune in, and drop out' disciples were especially fond of hallucinogenics. It was all bound to end in tears, and worse. If according to Don McLean's 'American Pie', the 2nd of February 1959 was the day the music (and life of Buddy Holly) died, then the 6th of December 1969 was the day the sixties died – three weeks early. On this day, the bottom fell out of the hippie era of peace and love, as The Rolling Stones' performance at the Altamont festival in southern California descended into an orgy of violence. Over-zealous 'policing' from the Hell's Angels resulted in the death of a young black man, who was brutally murdered not far from the stage. Mick

Jagger's pleas for the crowd to "cool it" went unheeded. The optimism generated by Woodstock scarcely a few months earlier was demolished as The Rolling Stones beat a hasty retreat. It could be argued that this was the day that the sixties stopped swinging.

RAMBLE ON

Ask any Joe Obvious who was the best guitarist in the history of popular music and the same old predictable suspects will be trotted out: Eric Clapton, Jimi Hendrix, Keith Richards, and Pete Townshend. However, there are other axe heroes who deserve special mention. Pink Floyd's David Gilmour knew how to pluck a few strings (as exemplified on 'Money', 'The Narrow Way', and Kate Bush's 'Wuthering Heights'). Mick Ronson, from Ziggy Stardust's Spiders From Mars provided dynamic guitar accompaniment in the glittering early years of David Bowie. Just take a listen to 'Moonage Daydream'.

Fast-forwarding to the eighties and nineties, The Edge from U2 has been a master of the six strings instrument, particularly during 'The Unforgettable Fire', and since. A couple of Manchester maestros are worthy of plaudits: namely John Squire from the Stone Roses (hailed by John Robb as the world's first non-macho guitar hero) and Noel Gallagher, whose guitar-playing probably eclipsed the highly-acclaimed Johnny Marr of The Smiths. However, the stand-out lead guitarist over the course of the last few decades is arguably Jimmy Page of Led Zeppelin.

Page was a hugely experienced session guitarist in the 1960s, before graduating after a spell in The Yardbirds into the role as axe man for the formidable Led Zeppelin. Page was also a sorely underrated producer and composer for the rock group, but it was his versatility as a blues guitarist ('Since I've Been Loving You'), acoustic guitarist ('Going To California', 'Poor Tom', and 'Black Mountain Side'), and rock guitarist ('Four Sticks' and 'Communication Breakdown') which collectively raises Page way beyond his contemporaries.

Such was the influence of Page and his group that they have spawned imitators on both sides of the Atlantic, too numerous to mention.

Jimmy Page, it is no secret, was a disciple of Aleister Crowley, with an unhealthy appetite for black magic. It has been suggested that the tragedies and bad vibes that have afflicted Led Zeppelin were attributable to Page's alleged pact with Lucifer. Well, I don't know the full truth of Jimmy Page's witchcraft, but he cast wonderful spells with his awesome guitar-playing. Perhaps it is true that the Devil has all the best tunes.

FREE NELSON MANDELA

There are few records that have impacted outside of the pop charts. One obvious exception is John Lennon's debut solo single 'Give Peace A Chance', famously recorded during a Montreal hotel bed-in in 1969, which became a great rallying cry for the anti-Vietnam War campaign. Similarly, John and Yoko's 'Happy Christmas (War Is Over)' was another anti-war anthem which struck a chord with thousands of people worldwide after its release in 1971.

Another 'historic' single which has never quite received the recognition that it merited was a track from a group by the name of The Special AKA, called 'Nelson Mandela'. Before this song squeezed into the Top Ten in early 1984, I had never heard of Robben Island's most famous 'resident'. I suspect that most of the post-sixties generation had never heard of this remarkable man who two decades earlier was the 'black pimpernel' – South Africa's public enemy number one. However, this song, the brainchild of Jerry Dammers (a sorely underrated composer and keyboardist) created greater awareness of the plight of Mandela in captivity and also of the sufferings of the black majority in the apartheid regime. Dammers assembled a host of artists, including ex-members of his former group The Specials, and The Beat, as well as recruiting Elvis Costello as producer for this rallying cry for the anti-apartheid movement.

Having never heard of Mandela before, I suddenly found this 'terrorist' being frequently mentioned on news items. Eventually, he was released in February 1990, and before long, this notorious 'criminal' became his country's President, impressing the world in his role as international statesman. An uptempo record from 1984 cannot be under-estimated in its impact upon Mandela's eventual release. Of course this ground-breaking single was dwarfed several months later when Bob Geldof and Midge Ure assembled an even more illustrious roster of pop artists to record the Band Aid single, 'Do They Know It's Christmas?', which was a worthy response to the news reports of famine in Ethiopia. Who knows, perhaps pop music can indeed change the world ... a little bit.

THE WEAKEST LINK

If you are an attention-seeker and you would like to make a fool of yourself on national television, and be humiliated by Anne Robinson, then write to the following address: Weakest Link, Freepost, BBC; or e-mail weakestlink@bbc.co.uk

MADCHESTER VERSUS MERSEYBEAT

I heard a bit of banter on Blokesport one Saturday night where Terry Christian and scouser Mick Quinn were arguing over the merits of the musical legacy of Lancashire's two big cities. The background to this 'debate' was the build-up to a Manchester United versus Liverpool football match. Well, I am going to steer clear of the issue of which football club is bigger, better, or has the most glorious history.

Sorry Mick, but I think that I can intrude on the musical legacy argument by stating that Manchester wins emphatically. Oh yes, one can stress the Mersey sound of the 1960s, but such Liverpool groups as

Gerry And The Pacemakers, Billy J Kramer And The Dakotas, and The Merseybeats looked and sounded awful in their dreadful suits, 'Beatle haircuts', and pop songs. As for the Fab Four, their best musical offerings came when they had fled south to the suburbs of London. The Brian Epstein stable produced formula pop that was as innovative and thought-provoking as a packet of crisps.

Manchester's groups however had a real edge to them. By-passing The Hollies and starting with The Buzzcocks and Joy Division in the 1970s, followed by New Order, The Smiths, the Happy Mondays and the Stone Roses in the 1980s, and finally Oasis in the 1990s, the city of Manchester can definitely exert bragging rights. As the northern capital of punk, new wave, and indie music, Madchester completely overshadows Liverpool and its legacy of Cilla Black, 'I Want To Hold Your Hand', and 'Ferry Cross The Mersey'.

SO YOU WANT TO BE A ROCK'N' ROLL STAR

Not only are the police getting younger every day, but I am becoming increasingly bored with the latest guitar heroes of the so-called indie scene: two indicators that I am growing old. Precisely what constitutes indie music is open to question. I will leave its definition in the semi-capable hands of the smart alecs of the music press. However, all I see is a musical landscape in which new guitar bands, equipped with their unshaven faces, semi-long hair, and anthems of angst about how rotten life is, simply re-cycle the same old formula. I find it all tiresome in the extreme. Has nobody ever told today's student heroes that there is a galaxy of different musical instruments to explore, such as sitar, harpsichord, organs, brass instruments, and strings? A fresh, original approach is required. Would-be indie heroes should try thinking outside of the box for a change. Ultimately, the Stone Roses were the original and best indie guitar group. Everything since, be it Snow Patrol or the Arctic Monkeys or whatever, is a pale imitation.

THE GREATEST-EVER BOY BAND SONGS

I always thought that a band was a group of musicians, so why do folk use this nonsense term of 'boy bands'? The singers in the boy bands are so talented that they have to disguise their voice in the midst of the other singers. I mean, if they are so good at singing, can they not sing on their own without the need for vocals from their co-dependent 'band' members? Anyhow, on the rest of this page, I have compiled a comprehensive list of what I consider to be the greatest-ever boy band tracks.

NOW THAT'S WHAT I CALL MUSIC

For all the great tracks of rock music, nothing quite 'rocks' the foundations of humanity like the most outstanding pieces of classical music. Personal favourites include Albinoni's Adagio for strings, Bach's 'Jesu joy of man's desire', Beethoven's Symphony No.7 allegretto, Handel's 'Berenice', and Mozart's clarinet concerto. However, I would like to throw a hat into the ring in the quest to find the world's greatest-ever piece of music. The candidate in question is 'The Sea' from Sheherazade by Rimsky-Korsakov. The word awesome is a much over-used adjective, but here it is perfectly appropriate.

A remarkable piece of music begins with percussion and strings frantically contributing to a fast-paced tempo. Then, the mood changes to a slower, more menacing sound, as brass instruments, assisted by a piccolo, take the composition in a different direction. Strings appear again as the track fades out, reminiscent of another nautical track, 'Echoes' by Pink Floyd, where there is a feeling of something disappearing over the horizon in the proceedings' conclusion. The change of pace in 'The Sea' is not unlike the alteration in tempo achieved on 'Strawberry Fields Forever' or the Floyd's 'Money'.

It is also to the credit of Rimsky-Korsakov that his composition is an accurate audio representation of the sea: violent, wild, and then peaceful and serene, yet always menacing in its beauty. There is a multitude of tracks in both classical and popular music which the reader may feel worthy of special mention, but as this is my project and it is intended to create discussion and provide food for thought, my own favourite, I believe, stands comparison with the greatest sounds in history.

'The Sea' from Sheherazade as performed by the Monte Carlo Philharmonic Orchestra is the kind of track that simply needs to be played at full volume to do justice to its majesty. Whether or not it is the world's best-ever piece of music is undoubtedly open to question, but only a Philistine would dare to disagree that they don't make them like this anymore.

ON MY RADIO

I concur with the words of 'On My Radio' by The Selecter. For the last two and a half decades, I have ignored radio in favour of playing my own albums, tapes, and compact discs. However, even I am growing a little tired of my own record collection. The trouble is that the terrifying alternative is to throw myself at the mercy of disc jockeys who deeply love the sound of their own voices and hope that in between their bouts of blowing hot air about nothing in particular they just might choose to play a listenable record. Some hope! Help is belatedly at hand as I have discovered a radio station called Chill on DAB digital radio where one can listen to a wide range of instrumentals and relaxing music, without suffering the accompanying baggage of trivia and gossip between songs. Chill is deejay-free and the music is all the better for it.

HANGING ON THE TELEPHONE

Everybody likes to receive telephone calls ... well, almost everybody. Indeed, it seems that many poor wretches have an uncontrollable urge to call someone on their mobile telephone every five minutes of the day. Well, I have mixed feelings when the telephone very occasionally rings. Rarely do I receive a pleasant telephone call, in which I am perhaps invited somewhere or the caller wants to share good news with me. Instead, my bitter memories of telephone calls are 'differences of opinion' with my family as well as bad news telephone calls. It is quite horrible when the telephone rings and you are informed that a parent has cancer. Then it rings another time and you are told that your loved one has two weeks to live. A subsequent telephone call reveals the worst possible 'news'. For every ten telephone calls that I have received, I could almost swear that about five or six have been unpleasant. The moral of this tale is quite simple. Unless you have something positive to say, then please don't upset me with another horrible telephone call. If there is anybody out there who has actually got something warm and pleasant to share with me, then your telephone call will be most welcome indeed. You can locate my number in the ex-directory.

HOW TO COPE WITH COLD CALLING

One of the most terrifying by-products of the advances in technology is the increasing volume of unwanted telephone calls from call centres. Having worked in such institutions, I am only too aware of the sheer joy (sic) that businesses and households derive from receiving unsolicited or 'cold' calls.

My humble advice to any unfortunate soul who receives a sales or marketing call is to ask the caller if he or she wouldn't mind being put on hold while the receiver tends to an apparently urgent matter, such as someone knocking on the front door. Then, just leave the caller on hold for a few minutes before he or she hangs up, as callers in call centres have targets to meet, and the last thing that the caller wants is to be detained on the same telephone call for too long. Callers also make notes of telephone calls, so give yourself the reputation of being someone who puts call centre sales agents on hold, to deter these nuisances from calling again.

Alternatively, ask the telephone sales executive (a ludicrous job title) for his or her own personal telephone number so that the sales agent can be telephoned out of the blue and given a dose of his or her own medicine. Whenever a caller asks for the receiver's personal details, such as an e-mail address, the receiver should only reveal this if the caller has agreed to supply his or her own address first.

Yes, receiving cold calls from 'gobby' twenty-somethings, fresh from university, is a menace, but hanging up is a spineless response. It is much more productive to play the call centre agents. They will soon tire of you, if you play the fool.

STAR TREATMENT AT THE CARPHONE WAREHOUSE

How appropriate that Carphone Warehouse should sponsor Pondlife Big Brother, a show in which four pieces of white trash practise the ancient English custom of bullying a foreigner. Rumour has it that Anonymity Big Brother will next be sponsored by the British National Party. As for Carphone Warehouse, well, they offer 'star treatment' according to their commercials, but the experience of many customers suggests otherwise.

Many people who have had the misfortune to be seduced (some might say, 'misled') by the promise of money back offers from Carphone Warehouse have discovered to their horror how many hoops that they have to leap through in order to claim back money from half line rental deals. For example, a customer is required to send in a 4th or 6th bill for his or her first redemption payment. However, it transpires that the required bill is number 5, not number 4, because Carphone Warehouse insist that they need the 4th airtime bill, which is bill number 5, and not bill number 4. You can imagine the confusion for many customers. If for some reason, the subsequent cheque fails to reach the customer, and he or she has to allow about fifty days for the cheque to arrive via Portugal, then a re-issued cheque is required, and a customer is expected to wait a further 60 to 80 days for the cheque. It can take many frustrating months for a customer to get their money 'redeemed'. Even a change of address for redemption claims is not mentioned to customers unless they happen to ring an advice line and find out, while little or no written information is available to help customers understand the redemption procedure. Furthermore, two claims for money back that are sent in the same envelope are treated as one claim with only one cheque being paid instead of two, while faxed or posted bills, that are missing a page are also rejected. Now, the question is, would you regard that as star treatment?

CAREER ADVICE

My humble advice to any youngsters with aspirations of a life of luxury and wealth is to try pursuing one of the following occupations: Marry Paul McCartney, and then divorce him a few years later, thereby winning a substantial compensation settlement for having to endure his singing on a daily basis. Alternatively, to those of an artistic inclination, why not paint a mural glorifying an Ulster terrorist group and then receive a generous donation from the government to remove your original artwork. Failing these enterprises, a career as a grossly overpaid footballer, golfer, tennis player, or a rock star is an absolute must. In the last resort, perhaps making a dishonest living as a television star would be desirable.

YOU CAN'T SEE THE WOOD FOR THE TREES

Dear reader, you know that you are a bandwagon-jumper, who can't see the wood for the trees if you think that Elton John's 'Don't Let The Sun Go Down On Me' or 'Candle In The Wind' is better than the hugely under-rated 'I've Seen That Movie Too' (from Goodbye Yellow Brick Road). Furthermore, you can't see the wood for the trees if you think that Eric Clapton's 'Wonderful Tonight' is a superior love song to the ace guitarist's 'Let It Grow'. Similarly, you can't see the wood for the trees if you think that'Wonderwall' or 'Don't Look Back In Anger' are better Oasis tracks than the sorely under-rated 'Columbia' (which is infinitely better than anything The Beatles ever did). Finally, you definitely cannot see the wood for the trees if you think that 'Nowhere To Run' by Martha Reeves and The Vandellas is a more appropriate Vietnam War track than The Byrds' 'Draft Morning', from their outstanding Notorious Byrd Brothers album.

Yes I know that tastes differ and beauty is in the eye of the beholder,but judging by how so many sheep shuffle in behind the 'humble' views of one or two critics, it is clear that a lot of people can't see the wood for the trees. There is a whole host of outstanding records out there that didn't get the credit that they deserve, while others are hyped beyond their worth. Perhaps the best examples are the tracks 'The Last Resort' and 'Pretty Maids All In A Row' which are considerably superior to The Eagles' 'Hotel California', while Simon And Garfunkel's 'The Only Living Boy In New York' is at least as good as 'Bridge Over Troubled Water'. Even Pink Floyd's 'obscure' album 'Obscured By Clouds' is nowhere near as inferior to its successor, 'The Dark Side Of The Moon', as some shallow experts would have you believe. Excuse my arrogance, ladies and gentlemen, but too many of you lovely people are swayed by the limited playlists and downright favouritism and neglect of numerous disc-jockeys.

Mind you, the worst culprits are the legion of Monty Python fans who draw attention to such highlights as the Lumberjack Song, the Dead Parrott sketch, or The Life Of Brian. It is patently obvious that these bandwagon-jumpers have not watched a single one of Flying Circus's forty-five 30 minute episodes. As I said, you just can't see the wood for the trees, especially the larch.

MONTY PYTHON'S FLYING CIRCUS

Nearly every October there is a documentary or newspaper article that celebrates the anniversary of the first reluctant BBC broadcast of a ground-breaking comedy show which Michael Palin wanted to be called Gwen Dibley's Flying Circus. The continual Transatlantic fascination with the pythons baffles me. They are horribly, nasty, slimy creatures. I much prefer cobras.

ABSOLUTELY MADNESS

I despair at the gradual erosion of what once constituted the proper use of the English language. Perhaps it is just symptomatic of a country whose citizens choose to be informed by tabloid rags, but I deplore those individuals who in growing numbers have substituted the phrase 'would have' with the wretchedly wrong 'would of'. It is a damning indictment that many foreigners and immigrants (there is a difference) speak considerably better English than Joe Tabloid and many other supposedly 'true' English people.

Worse still is the tendency among most people (educated or otherwise) to pepper their statements with a plethora of absolutes. For example, when you say "never", do you truly mean: not once, on any single occasion? Similarly, when you use the word "always", do you really mean: every single time, without exception? Furthermore, I frequently hear the word "everybody" being misused and abused. Surely you don't mean every single person, whilst "nobody" implies absolutely no-one in the world. There are exceptions to every rule, which therefore renders the use of this absolutist terminology obsolete. The trouble is of course that we tend to use absolutes when we are prone to exaggerate. It is however a violation of the English language, and I hope that everybody pays attention to this English lesson, and I never want to hear the use of absolutes again – from nobody.

IN THE NAME OF GOD

One of the massive ironies of human history during the last two millennia is that such phenomena as the Crusades, the thoroughly unpleasant Spanish Inquisition, the religious wars in Europe in the sixteenth century, the English Civil War, the religious conflict in Ireland and Scotland in the seventeenth century, to name but a few, were all perpetrated in the name of God. The participants in all this bloodshed along with the noble savages who drove the Africans, the Aboriginies, and the Red Indians off their native territories will be perhaps shocked to discover on Judgment Day that their Creator is far from happy with the blood, misery, pain, and torture inflicted apparently in His name. I have been reliably informed that the last act of violence that was acceptable to God was the sacrifice of His son on the cross in AD 30. Those Christian, Jewish, or Muslim 'fanatics' who have subsequent to this date attempted to justify their murders as being God-sponsored are sadly mistaken.

LOSING MY RELIGION

I grew up a Protestant. Like most people in this wonderful world, my religious affiliation was inherited at birth, and not the result of an informed choice from all the available 'brands'. I no longer consider myself a Protestant. My 'road to Damascus' moment was when so-called Protestants in Northern Ireland gunned down a young Roman Catholic postman a few years ago for no other apparent reason than he was a fenian who dared to date a Protestant, and thus 'contaminate' her. The shame of him. Worse still were the so-called Protestants who blocked youngsters en route to primary school, not to mention those lovely Christians who picketed the Roman Catholic church at Harryville, Ballymena. What a lot of people do not realize is that the word 'protestant' derives from the fact that in the 1520s, some early followers of the theology of Martin Luther made a declaration in which they proclaimed or 'protested' their faith. The trouble is that ever since, they have been protesting against everybody else's faith. Surely the Protestant loyalists of Northern Ireland are not the modern representatives of Martin Luther, let alone the ambassadors of Jesus Christ.

I have also become increasingly disenchanted with the loyal orders, so-called. I admit that I have got a kick out of parading along the middle of the road behind various bands, and if they are honest, other 'Christian' loyalists ought to admit the same. Parading however is just an ego exercise in which thousands of n'er-do-wells feel like they are king for a day, swapping their blue collar jobs for their Sunday best, as they wave at all their family and friends. Let's face it, the word 'parading' basically means showing off, or in the case of Ulster loyalists, it is a thinly disguised show of strength to their neighbours. A Glaswegian once told me that an orange parade in his city was just an outing for Glasgow's underclass. These 'Christian' loyalists seem to think that Protestantism is a badge of pride in which former glorious battles are celebrated. However, the sectarian murders in Ulster, not to mention the numerous killings in Europe since the sixteenth century would suggest that there is much shame attached with Protestantism. Protestants were just as responsible as Roman Catholics for the various outbreaks of anti-semitism in Europe over the last few centuries.

Where the biblical precedent is for loyalist parades, I have never located in frequent searches. There is nothing in the life and teachings of Jesus Christ to resemble the practice of triumphalist parades. The nearest the Lord came to 'parading' was riding into Jerusalem on a donkey, followed shortly after by exiting the city with a cross. Why on God's earth do so-called Christians have to march behind drums en route to worship at God's house? It is pseudo-militaristic nonsense, which distorts Christianity. It is as if too many people are consumed by one particular Christian hymn, which states " onward Christian soldiers, marching as to war". Just to prove how 'Christian' the loyalists of Ulster really are will be their predictably hostile, 'Christian' response to my Lundy-like treachery.

What is even more baffling is the reluctance of Unionist politicians to share power with former terrorists. Forgiveness is at the epicentre of Christianity. Did Jesus Christ not forgive his executioners whilst he languished on the cross? Only forgiven people (by God) can forgive. Those 'Christians' who cannot or will not forgive their erstwhile enemies are clearly not forgiven (or saved) people, as they frequently seem to suggest. Some people's Christian outlook is a distinctively selective one. Loyalists should take a leaf out of the book of Gordon Wilson (whose daughter was tragically killed in the Enniskillen war memorial bomb in November 1987). Gordon Wilson can forgive the murderers of his Mary, which makes him a thousand times more worthy follower of Jesus Christ than the Ulster Protestants who don't forgive.

Of all the loyal orders, the Royal Black Preceptory is the least controversial one. For the sake of simplicity, it is basically a cross between the Orange Order and the freemasons, with perhaps a stronger emphasis on biblical scriptures than the Orange Order or the Apprentice Boys of Derry. However, the Black Institution requires its 'Sir Knights' (a ludicrous form of address) to complete eleven degrees which contain 37 Old Testament references and a paltry eleven New Testament references. Therefore, with 75% of degree work based on the Old Testament, the Royal Black Preceptory seems to focus more on Judaism than on Christianity. Consequently, God is severely mis-represented by this pick-n-mix approach to his Word. Most alarming of all, only three of the 48 biblical references are drawn from the four New Testament gospels. This is scarcely compelling evidence of an organisation focusing on their Lord and Saviour, Jesus Christ. Yet, central to the Christian faith is the realisation that no-one comes to the Father except through the Son. It seems to me that Ulster loyalists like to fuse and even confuse worship of God with adoration of the Queen, yet God reminds us that he refuses to tolerate any 'competitors' or idols, while it would be important for the loyal orders to remember that Jesus Christ is the King of kings. Every other monarch, be it Elizabeth II, William III or whoever is a pale imitation. It is my humble opinion therefore that the loyal orders and 'Christian', God-fearing loyalists of Ulster are skating on extremely thin ice!

CHRISTIANITY

Most young people would do very well to discard their posters and adulation of flawed, unreliable heroes, pin-ups, and 'stars', and focus on the flawless, totally reliable saviour Jesus Christ. While we all let people down at various times of our lives, without necessarily meaning to do so, the Messiah fails nobody. Christianity is a good thing. What spoils it is Christians. Like many people, when I hear someone with a Northern Irish accent starting to rant about God, I want to run for cover.

HEAVEN

It is remarkable how everybody who dies seems destined for heaven, if funeral services and posthumous tributes for every dead person are anything to go by. Yes it is absolutely amazing that people who think that Moses and David are New Testament characters are apparently heaven-bound. The reality, I'm afraid, is a lot different. Sorry to be a party-pooper folks, but there are thousands, even millions of people in denial about the eternal destination of nice old Uncle Fred or kind old Auntie Mary. Just who will be feasting at God's great banquet then? Well, heaven will include many Africans, many Asians, Latin Americans, South Americans, even North Americans, not to mention Germans, French, Italians, even Australians. Therefore, any xenophobic white supremacist 'Christian' should come to terms with the fact that God is preparing a home for repentant sinners from all corners of the world from all walks of life, including solicitors and maybe even journalists too.

SURRENDER

In Northern Ireland surrender is a dirty word for both communities. The Apprentice Boys of Derry annually commemorate the thirteen citizens of Derry who exclaimed no surrender and shut the gates of their city on the troops of their king, James II in December 1688. As a consequence, the brave citizens of Derry were subjected to a 105 day siege during which starvation threatened to cause more suffering than the soldiers outside the city walls. Ever since, Ulster protestants (and Irish republicans too) have regarded the word surrender as a euphemism for capitulation and defeat.

However, there are times when surrender is the only option. One such example was the fall of France in June 1940. Newly-appointed British Prime Minister, Winston Churchill, flew across the English Channel and pleaded in tears with his beleaguered allies to carry on the fight, but such was the overwhelming success of the German army's blitzkrieg that surrender was truly unavoidable. I think that I too have reached the point of surrender. All my hopes and dreams are disappearing one by one. I am surrounded by people who do not appreciate me or understand me. For my part, there is scarcely anyone outside of my family circle, who I admire and respect. I simply don't like what I see and what I hear. Precious little amuses me. Plenty more bores and irritates me. My family and friends (like Churchill before them) must accept the realities of my defeat and humiliation. In a society where my peers and contemporaries cannot see the wood for the trees, this big lump of wood has rotted long enough. I am far more talented than most entertainers and scribes put together, but nobody believed in me. I never was in the right place at the right time, and I have not moved in the right circles where doors open for me. Forgive my self-pity, but I feel truly marginalised.

I do not advocate suicide to anyone. Let's make that abundantly clear. However, to the Northern Irish protestants, I urge you brothers to come out with your hands up and surrender, yes surrender to your king, Jesus Christ.

THE KINGDOM OF GOD

It is vastly ironic that 250 years ago, America was a colony of the British Empire, while nowadays Britain is a colony of the American Empire. History ancient and modern is a chronicle of the rise and fall of numerous empires, be it the Eqyptians, the Greeks, the Romans, the Incas, the Spanish, the French, the British, the Nazis, or the Soviet Union. Those peoples who have suffered under the oppressive yolk of imperialistic conquest and occupation should console themselves that all mighty empires in the story of mankind are essentially castles made of sand. Only the kingdom of God will prove infinitely durable than all the once-great empires, because unlike them, it is not founded on fear and terror.

THE WILL OF GOD

Regardless of how many personal demons each of us may or may not possess, all our lives are a constant battle between what we want and what God wants. Many Christians and church-goers frequently state "Thy will be done" in the Lord's prayer, but just how many of us, Christian and otherwise, actually allow God's will to be done, or realised. I concede that God is an all-powerful being who can do whatever He chooses and He can make or break us, if He wishes. However, God in His grace has provided us with free will, empowering His creation with the decision to either submit to His will in the expectation that our loving Father knows what is best for us, or alternatively we can choose to walk our own path, paved with our wants and desires and do our own thing.

For me, I am very conscious of a remarkable story from the Old Testament book of Numbers in which Balaam sets out on a journey to Balak, king of Moab, on his donkey. God in this instance sends an angel, oblivious to Balaam, to block the donkey's route and warn it to not advance. Consequently, Balaam is enraged when his faithful ass wanders off the road. The donkey is given the power of speech and explains to Balaam that it would be unwise for him to defy God's will and complete his journey. Jonah and Paul the great evangelist also intended to make journeys, contrary to God's will, resulting in Jonah being held captive inside a whale until he came to his senses, while Paul was executed in Rome before he was able to travel to Spain. In the latter story, God was satisfied with Paul's work as an apostle and his extra journey was not necessary.

Like Jonah sulking inside the whale and Balaam making an ass of himself, I too have struggled to submit to the will of God. I have tried to make journeys which God hasn't approved of. However, I am slowly coming round to the realisation that God is the best possible navigator whose will should be done and that resistance to God is futile.

THE 'WRATH' OF GOD

I concede that by dividing my project into an Old Testament and a New Testament, and including Genesis, Exodus, and Revelations, I have sailed a bit close to the wind. Nevertheless, I believe that God has a sense of humour and will forgive my risqué remarks. I still wouldn't be the slightest surprised if hordes of placard-carrying, God-fearing Christians besiege my humble abode.

I remain a little baffled as to why certain Christians describe themselves as 'God-fearing'. Someone who declares that he or she is 'saved' has presumably been forgiven, and consequently saved from the wrath of God. It is hugely ironic that the atheists and heathen who have rejected Jesus Christ as their Lord and Saviour do not fear God, whilst those who claim to be Christians fear Him. This does not make a morsel of sense. Walking with God requires someone to have a personal relationship with Jesus Christ, the King of kings. However, there is something unhealthy about a relationship that is built on fear. Anyone who feared their parents or spouse will testify that the relationship was not a warm and loving one. A real relationship with the Messiah is not founded on fear, and anyone who describes themselves as God-fearing needs a re-think. What precisely is it that they fear?

ELIJAH AND THE PROPHETS OF BAAL

Whether or not you are a practising Christian or Jew, you will be familiar with such Old Testament stories as Noah and The Ark, the crossing of the Red Sea (which was in reality the Sea of Reeds), Samson and Delilah, and David and Goliath. As an amateur Bible scholar, I readily admit that certain books of the Old Testament are more readable than others. However, I would like to highlight a biblical epic that has never received the attention that it deserves.

This is the story of the 'contest' between Jewish prophet Elijah and the idolatrous 400 prophets of Baal.

In this true story, the 'competitors' agreed to make a sacrifice to their respective God to ascertain which God would respond. The 400 prophets built a fire and awaited Baal to magically light the flames. No such action was forthcoming, and the idolaters started to rant and rave, cutting themselves until the blood flowed, exhorting Baal to respond. In a rare moment of Biblical humour, Elijah urged his adversaries to shout louder, suggesting that perhaps Baal is asleep, day-dreaming, or even relieving himself! Elijah then took to the stage, in a manner of speaking, and when he offered his sacrifice to Heaven, the one and only God responded with fire, proving to the startled onlookers that Baal was no alternative to the Creator of the earth.

Aside from the hint of humour, I am inspired by a story where one man opposed the views of 400 'know it alls' and won. In our society, 'the greater number' holds sway. Elections are decided by the greater number and minorities have found themselves marginalised. However, you should not be mistaken for thinking that just because many more people disagree with you or dress differently from you does not make them right and you wrong. Most 'small' people take the easy option and follow the crowd, but going with the flow can be dangerous. Not for nothing did Jesus Christ state that the way to salvation and eternal life is a narrow one. Crowd-followers must think for themselves. It was not so long ago that the Nazis were actually voted into power in 1932. If a lot of people share the same view, it does not automatically follow that this view is correct. To those who embrace Christianity or at the very least are prepared to take a stand against the numerous voices around them, I salute you.

For the uninitiated, this remarkable story can be found by reading the First Book of Kings. Please do not be afraid to browse through the Bible. As Mr O'Daniel in the film 'Midnight Cowboy' urged Joe Buck: "don't run from Jesus".

THE LAST WORD

Why are so many people scared or embarrassed by the name Jesus? The very same people who deny the Saviour are the same misguided souls who take his name in vein on frequent occasions. Mind you, the Saviour's thoughts, words, and actions also frightened people in Palestine 2000 years ago. Many bystanders walked away in sadness or perhaps fear when the Lord exhorted them to follow Him. Jesus Christ in human form was a remarkable superman, combining a plethora of roles: carpenter, fisherman, healer, preacher, servant, teacher, and saviour. When He observed people deserting Him, the Lord asked His disciples, "would you too like to leave?", to which Peter replied: "Lord, to whom would we go?" Dear reader, to whom can you go?

EXODUS (HAPPY ENDING)

If you are glancing through this book in the bookshop and you happen to have opened this page, then yes I will reveal that all the crimes committed in this publication were perpetrated predictably by the butler. So there you go, mystery solved.

If you have been overwhelmed by the insights and profound wisdom of this self-proclaimed, misunderstood genius, then I shall proceed to mercifully put you out of your misery. Speaking of misery, it occurred to me one day whilst out jogging that life is like running around an athletics track. We run round in circles ad nauseam and then suddenly we stop, pure and simple. There is no happy ending yet to my story because I am still chasing elusive dreams. Still, without hope or faith, life is empty. It only remains for me to say that if you have enjoyed digesting my food for thought half as much as I have enjoyed dishing it out, then I have enjoyed it twice as much as you.

So please kindly close the book, pick up your belongings, don't leave your umbrella behind, and quietly leave without disturbing the neighbours. I cannot begin to say how grateful that I am that you decided to pay me a visit. Do feel free to call again. Now safe journey home, and drive carefully. Auf wiedersehen, pets.

REVELATIONS

Hindsight is a wonderful thing, I agree, but foresight is infinitely more useful. Whilst exiled on the penal colony of Ireland, the following visions of the future were revealed to me: Chelsea Football Club enjoy world domination until 2021 when new European giants Mansfield Town (owned by a Texas oil baron) win the Champions League and achieve the domestic treble. Mansfield's meteoric rise to success is eclipsed a couple of years later by Accrington Stanley (a team that includes no fewer than eight Brazilian internationals, purchased by their consortium of drug dealers, pop stars, and sheikhs).

I am delighted to announce that England re-gain the coveted Ashes in 2013 when those oh so humble Australians (bored with their ritual humiliations of the Poms) send over an under 12s team of girls to ensure an evenly contested series. Regrettably, England's possession of the Ashes is rudely interrupted in 2034 when Australia recall Shane Warne from an old folks' home, whilst Glenn McGrath in crutches returns to torment England's hapless batsmen. Ricky Ponting also re-gains his place in the team when his appeal for parole is successfully upheld.

Meanwhile in the world of athletics, British competitors in the 2012 London Olympic Games are granted a fifty metres head start to appease the demands of Britain's new tyrant, President Brown. Time and space does not permit me to detail England football team's World Cup adventures, but suffice to say that the words quarter-finals, penalty kicks, Portugal, and Germany give you some indication of the national team's fate. Also, in Six Nations rugby union, Ireland finally achieve the grand slam in 2025 when the French team are locked in their dressing room at half-time, and thus forced to forfeit their match, leaving Ireland with the formality of clinching the clean sweep at

Twickenham where they record their twenty-second successive victory over England. Finally, in the wacky world of Ryder Cup golf, it is mutually agreed that the European team play in blindfolds in 2022 to allow the Americans an opportunity to eventually re-gain the trophy.

I warn everyone who hears the words of the prophecy of this book: If anyone adds anything to them ,God will add to him the plagues described in this book. And if anyone takes words away from this book of prophecy, God will take away from him his share in the tree of life and in the holy city, which are described in this book.

He who testifies to these things says "Yes, I am coming soon." Amen. Come, Lord Jesus. The grace of the Lord Jesus be with God's people. Amen. (Extract from Revelations, Chapter 22)

ROLL THE CREDITS

Modern movies rarely manage to impress this once impressionable young man. Amongst other things, there is a growing trend for credits to go on ad infinitum, or at least ad nauseam. It's a less than subtle way of the movie-makers reinforcing the fact that they have gone to an enormous amount of effort and expense to stage their epic, which ought to be nominated for an Oscar. Oh yeah? Well, I have a terrifying vision of the future in which we will be watching a thirty-minute movie, followed by an hour and a half of 'credits'.

Furthermore, I have never understood the public fascination with all those wonderful, superior film stars out there. Most 'stars' are dull, boring people. People queuing at my local bus stop are infinitely more interesting than most film actors. The 'chicks' at the local supermarket check-outs are better looking than most models. The regulars at my local pub are better singers than most pop idols, while many of my relatives and friends are considerably funnier than most so-called comedians. Why are so many people in awe of celebrities? These lucky and un-deserving prima donnas don't posses a tiny fraction of my talents.

Anyhow, this publication was conceived in the back of a car and written entirely by me, so you don't have to issue arrest warrants or straitjackets to anyone else. Also, no animals were hurt in the making of this epic – just a few trees.

My make-up artist was David Blunkett
My wardrobe – Full of old clothes
My window-cleaner – Reg Gumby
My milkman – Ernie (the fastest in the west)
My baker – Two Ton Ted from Teddington
My psychiatrist – Arthur Putey
My social worker – Robyn Andersson
My hairdresser – Audrey Roberts
My heroin supplier – Peter Dockerty

My travel agent – Mr Smoketoomuch
My next-door neighbour – Ned Flanders
My role model – Barney Gumble
My bodyguard – Adrian McLeister
My stunt double – Terry Clarke
My accountant – Mr Anchovy
My mortgage advisor – Gerard Wiley
My general practitioner – Dr. Strangelove
My chiropodist – Mrs. Pepperpot
My parents – Mummy And Daddy
My grandparents – Granny and Grandad, and Granny and Grandad
My postman – Martin Lockrey
My mechanic – Kevin Webster
My pub landlord – Al Murray
My car dealer – George Nearly
My newsagent – Norris Cole
My solicitor – Richard Lewis
My gasman – James Robert Morrison
My dentist – David Lucas
My private investigator – Jim Rockford
My imaginary girlfriend – Charlotte Ross
My boyfriend – Julian Clearly
My housekeeper – Mrs Doyle
My babysitter – Vicky Pollard
My cardio-thoracic surgeon – Connie Beecham
My chauffeur – Dennis Patterson
My parish priest – Father Ted Crilly
My vicar – The Very Reverend David Lyndhurst
My manager – Claudio Ranieri
My sovereign – Lizzie Windsor
My demons – Too numerous to mention
My Enemy – Satan
My Creator – God
My Saviour and Lord – Jesus Christ

This book was written on location at Pinewood, Shepperton, Ealing, Hollywood, Bangkok, Copenhagen, Miami, New York, and Rochdale.

ABBREVIATIONS

AA: AA stands for Alcoholics Anonymous. If you ever pay a visit to Egypt to see the pyramids, you will also find many drunkards languishing in the local river, as those with a drink problem start their road to recovery in denial. What I don't understand about the AA is that if they wish to remain anonymous, then why do they produce television commercials, attempting to sell car insurance? AA also means the Automobile Association. I once made an embarrassing visit to a local meeting of the Automobile Association where I immediately plucked up the courage to get up on my feet and confess that I am a drunk. Well, it got several laughs, if nothing else.

BBC: According to George Galloway, it means the Blair and Bush Corporation. 'The Very Best Of Monty Python's Flying Circus' (Methuen, 2006) suggests that it is the Bloody Bigots Club. There is a less plausible alternative that BBC stands for the British Broadcasting Corporation, which obliges the nation to pay increased license fees to finance such impoverished millionaire presenters as Jonathan Woss.

IRA: Ireland's Richest Assassins. Sinn Fein is rumoured to be one of Europe's richest political parties. Its members deny that the organisation benefits from the proceeds of republican crime, such as the Northern Bank Raid, yet the party rarely feels the need to hold jumble sales for fundraising.

MBE: Monstrously Big Egos. If England cricketers are honoured by Her Satanic Majesty (sorry, Her Britannic Majesty) for narrowly squeezing home in an Ashes series, then should it not logically follow that good Queen Bess send Freddie And The Dreamers to the

Tower of London for the whitewash abomination of 2006-2007 at the hands of those bad winners, Australia.

MP: Mad Person. The House of Commons can have more than 650 such, unsupervised mad persons. If they are particularly mad, they are returned to this asylum to serve an extra four or five years. Those who aren't mad enough are released after four or five years. Very mad people like Winston Churchill and Edward Heath were so mad that they were sent to this Bedlam for many decades. MP also means Military Police, those brave soldiers who spend their war-time dodging the fighting by going around and arresting anybody else who is dodging the fighting.

PIG: People in general. Britain's people in general are half-educated binge drinkers who like nothing more than to exaggerate, swear, read tabloids and watch reality tv and soaps.

SAS: Shoot all suspects. The SAS has many mottoes, one of which is shoot dead first, and interrogate the corpse second.

SHIT: Co-founded by George Dubya Bush and his faithful lapdog Tony Blair, this is the Society for Hunting International Terrorists.

THFC: Totally Hopeless Football Club. They occasionally play football at White Hart Lane and their supporters still harbour delusions of grandeur, based on league trophies won more than forty years ago. Their self-importance is all the more surprising when you consider that of the six English clubs that have competed in a European final between 1984 and 2006, not one was toothless Tottenham. Also, of the thirteen different FA Cup finalists between 1992 and 2006, not one was Totally Hopeless, while of the eleven league champions since 1963 not one of them is the mythically mighty Spurs.

UDA: Unemployed Drug Addicts. Since peace has broken out those courageous loyalist terrorists who used to gun down unarmed Roman Catholics have had to seek a career making an honest living in betting shops each afternoon to supplement their state benefits. In their spare time, loyalist terrorists love nothing more than a nice walk in the summer ... behind a band.

DISCLAIMER

Neither the author nor the publishing company wish to condone the dreadful act of suicide, but if after reading this book, you have lost the will to live, well that's your funeral.

AN APOLOGY (TO THE BBC)

The author and publishers would like to issue their collective heartfelt regrets that they pillaged an excerpt from 'Blackadder Goes Forth' without the kind permission of the BBC. The author is Adam Ant that he submitted a request by post, and he is desperately keen that his perceived lack of courtesy causes no offence. However, he warns that should the BBC express its disapproval at his violation of publishing etiquette, then he will cease watching Holby City in retaliation. If the BBC chooses to take legal action, the author will merely urge his family, fans, and friends to cancel their television license direct debits as a reprisal. Happy New Year,

K.J. Rolling, April 1st 2007

DON'T GIVE UP THE DAY JOB

As an extra special treat, I have included a prized extract from a recent performance of mine on the London leg of my world (Don't) Comeback tour, so–called because I was warned after each show to never return – until I have something amusing to say. Anyhow, here goes:

"Good evening, ladies and gentlemen, boys and girls. Our opening hymn tonight is number 862. Gosh you are so well-behaved and half asleep – like a Church of England congregation. Actually, I must say that it is a real thrill for me to be here. It was either this or stay at home, watch Emmerdale, followed by Eastenders, and then cry myself to sleep. For those one or two of you in the audience who don't know who

I am, I was short-listed for Oscars several years ago. They're a wine bar in Stoke-on-Trent who were looking for staff. Don't laugh please. It only encourages me. Seriously though, I am here by public demand. The regulars at my local pub demanded that I go and irritate people in another pub instead ... This is supposed to be a talent night, but I am struggling to spot any talent whatsoever. I have already counted 37 unattractive people, and that doesn't include the bar staff. Otherwise the figure goes up to 45. There are however benefits in being ugly – so they tell me. For example, nobody wants to sit next to you on the bus, so you have two seats for the price of one. Oh you lucky lucky people. Sometimes I wish that I was unattractive. Do you want to hear something really funny? About time too, I hear you say. You lot have paid a fiver here tonight to listen to me. I think that's hilarious. You obviously don't ... Have you ever noticed the comedians who have not prepared any material whatsoever? About two or three minutes into their performance, they descend into "where you from?", "where you from?" ... So, where are you from? You sir in the red shirt. The only reason that I want to know is because I find you very attractive. Don't worry. I don't want to have a relationship with you. Just sex...nothing complicated ... I can tell that you are sorely tempted. He's thinking to himself 'that's the last time I ever sit in the front row anywhere'......You have all been such a lovely audience that I would like to take you all home with me. You can sleep in the garden. Don't think that I am letting any of you into my house. I share a home with a drug addict, a football hooligan, and a prostitute. There is no way that I am letting you lot in my house. You would lower the tone. Before I return later on with an encore, during which I will be humming two tracks from my new album, I would like to finish with a friendly piece of advice. Don't drink and drive – at least not tonight, because later on I have to cross the road outside, and I don't want any of you alcoholics driving along at the time. In my defence I only agreed to appear tonight because all the other comedians demanded someone who would make them seem funny and talented. Well, thank you very much for suffering me. Give yourselves a round of applause. You've earned it."

ESSAY QUESTION

Angry blokes can disturb everyone from going home in jolly kind lorries, making noise or perhaps quietly running sideways towards underground verandas with xenophobic young zoologists. Discuss.

FICTION OR NON-FICTION

As part of this book was ghost written by Jeffrey Archer (sic), you are clearly feeling a bit baffled as to which remarks in this volume are true and which are written in jest. Here is a little exercise for you to differentiate between which statements are fact and which are fiction:

1 I was in Parkhurst.

2 Clement Attlee's conversion sealed a 13–12 win for Widnes against the Munich Brownshirts in the 1932 rugby league Challenge Cup Final at Wembley.

3 I am a comic genius.

4 I worked briefly as a male prostitute for the Conservative Parliamentary Party.

5 Jimmy Greaves scored the only goal of the game in England's goalless draw with Uruguay in 1966.

6 I was in Rampton hospital, briefly.

7 I am a hugely talented writer.

8 Sean Connery narrowly failed to qualify for the Men's Singles at Wimbledon in 1961.

9 I was born in Yorkshire in the 1960s, during an episode of Heartbeat.

10 I am a misfit.

11 I have spoken frequently to the Samaritans.

12 I am a former member of the Apprentice Boys of Derry.

13 I applied for a job, driving a getaway car in a bank raid.

14 Ronnie Corbett failed by only one stroke to qualify for the 1964 British Open golf tournament.

15 I am 432nd in line of succession to the throne of Belgium.

16 I was persuaded away from the edge of the roof by two policemen.

17 Adolf Hitler was offended by Jesse Owens's black power salute after he won the 100 metres butterfly at the 1936 Munich Olympic Games.

18 I am an outstanding singer.

19 My family was the only household in our council estate that didn't own a gun.

20 Salman Rushdie scored an own goal in Scotland's 1-1 draw with Iran at the 1978 World Cup finals.

21 Jeffrey Archer came a commendable fourth in the 50 kilometres hurdles at the 1969 Stockholm Commonwealth Games.

22 I have auditioned for a couple of bands.

23 I have appeared on Countdown.

24 Linford Christie has three testicles.

25 Jonathan Woss is grossly under-paid by the BBC.

(Answers on page 189)

MUSIC QUIZ

Since you have all been such good sports and bought (and even read) my book, I will treat you to a little music quiz. Can you lovely people name the recording artists for the following tracks which I have used as titles for some of my fabulous pieces:

Another Brick in the Wall
Ashes to Ashes
Born Slippy
Drive My Car
Exodus
God Save The Queen
Hanging on the Telephone
I'm Still Waiting
In the Summertime
Left to My Own Devices
Losing My Religion
Mistletoe and Wine
On My Radio
Police and Thieves
Ramble On
Rush Hour
Smalltown Boy
So You Want to be a Rock' n' Roll Star
Stop Your Sobbing
Surrender
Tears of a Clown
The Lonely Crowd
The Times They Are a-Changin'
Thieves Like Us
Uncle Sam
Wasted Life
Welcome to My World
What's Another Year?

If you are unsure of any of the answers, drop me a line via e-mail and I will furnish you with the correct answers.

INDEX

AN INTERVIEW WITH THE AUTHOR

If there is any justice, my publication will prompt numerous magazines, newspapers, radio, and television shows to seek an interview with me to challenge me to defend the indefensible (material of my book). In the absence of such interrogation, I have constructed one here to justify my work of outstanding beauty.

Interviewer: What possessed you to write this book?

Author: Demons, pure and simple. No seriously, the roots of this book can be traced back a few years to when I went to London to have a bash, among other things, at stand-up comedy. I made a handful of appearances, nothing remarkable, just five minute slots in front of an enthusiastic, heckler-free audience. As well as being an exercise in character-building (or sado-masochism, more particularly), I rather hoped that someone with a cigar in his mouth, wearing a long coat would approach me at the end of my 'show', put his hand on my shoulder and promise "young man, I've got big plans for you". Mind you, as a Christian, I think that God has done just this, although I scarcely believe that a showbiz career in stand-up comedy is what He has in mind. I did get a generous reception from the audiences with various laughs, but as London is saturated with comedy clubs featuring a welter of funny people more laughable than me, I awoke to the reality that my 'stage career', like my other careers, was going nowhere slowly. I passionately believed in my product, but I don't think that as a novice, not to mention nervous, performer that I did it full justice. I might be better served supplying my material to more accomplished 'entertainers' (if the price is right), but I still felt that I had pieces that I should expose. Gosh, that doesn't sound right.

I toyed with the idea of recording myself on tape, irritating the listener with an hour's monologue of my supposed comedy gems. Instead of which, I hit upon the fantastic idea of writing a book based on my humorous observations and rants. However, after including such world-renowned repertoire as 'Paris', 'Thieves Like Us', and 'Vetting', I realised I did not have enough to fill a book, so I ventured off into non-humorous rants. Then, when I inspected my growing army of comments and observations, my conscience reared its ugly head and cautioned me that there was arguably so much negativity, and perhaps anger or even bitterness, that I ought to use the book as a vehicle to share on a positive note, my Christian faith. I also included dollops of satire and a teaspoonful of my passion for sport and a table-spoonful of my passion for popular music, sprinkling my piece de resistance with history and politics and my passion for women (which may not necessarily be mutual). Voila, here we have it. My recipe for literary acclaim, or disaster. Delete as appropriate. Sorry for the long and winding road of an answer, but you did ask, so you've only got yourself to blame. Hey, wake up and ask me another question.

Interviewer: Do you not think that the title of 'How To Commit Suicide In Ten Easy Steps' is likely to cause offence or at least scare people away from handing it to the assistant in a bookshop?

Author: I readily admit that 'How To Commit Suicide In Ten Easy Steps' is a controversial choice for a title, but I have stressed two or three times in the book that I do not approve of suicide. Of course, the subject is especially raw for many families touched by such a tragedy, and I myself was quite close to a young woman who took her own life at the tender age of 27. I am not trying to make light of the concept of suicide, but I regard my choice of title as an illustration of my own sense of black humour. Furthermore, I was feeling rather down in the dumps myself when I began this whole project, so the suicide title is really a poke at myself. After all, my next preferred choice of title was 'Losing The Will To Live'. Besides, I elected to adopt such an eye-catching title because in a bookshop, I am competing for attention against hundreds of excellent books, renowned authors and celebrities, so I reserve the right to use shock tactics to ensure that my publication receives maximum exposure. When all is said and done, I do not expect a single soul to end his or her life on account of my apparent 'advice'.

Interviewer: You divide your publication peculiarly into an Old Testament and a New Testament, featuring pieces entitled 'Genesis', 'Exodus', and 'Revelations'. Would you not agree that you are sailing a bit close to the wind?

Author: Yes, some of my work is a bit risqué, not to mention risky. I could not however resist the temptation (devil-induced?) to split my book into an Old Testament and a New Testament, believing myself to be the first person in human history to do so since God, so I am in pretty good company! It is really just an exercise in mischief-making, and I do not believe that God will be beside himself with rage. I will actually let you into a little secret: God has a sense of humour, so why can't Father and son have a little light-hearted craic? My earthly father and me engaged in various leg-pulling banter, so why should my relationship with the true Special One be any different?

Yes, I will be accused of irreverence, not to mention blasphemy, but if dividing my publication into a Genesis, Exodus, Revelations, Old Testament, and New Testament is all that I have to worry about, then I am even more of a good and faithful servant than I previously realised. The trouble is that too many 'God-fearing' Christians do the Creator a massive injustice by portraying Him as angry, disapproving, hard to please, stern, with a zero tolerance of anyone and everyone. Now I'm not suggesting that our Father in Heaven, hallowed be His name, is a dope-smoking liberal, but it is the misconception of our loving Father which scares non-believers away from Christianity. Most non-believers shy away from Jesus Christ because they have erroneously decided that they are not good enough, yet the paradox is that God wants to have a relationship with flawed people. The Messiah after all came to earth two thousand years ago and befriended lepers and outcasts, not godly believers. Anyhow, I digress.

Interviewer: Is it not a bit incongruous to write a book entitled 'How To Commit Suicide In Ten Easy Steps', with scathing remarks about various individuals and organisations, and yet finish with various references to your Christian faith?

Author: Yes, I do make unkind remarks at various points, but I am also very self-critical too. Let's make that clear. Quite frankly, if I had written a book entitled 'How To Find God In Ten Easy Steps', such a publication would be confined to the shelves of a Christian bookshop, being bought and read only by fellow-Christians. Christian books and testimonies are almost exclusively read by fellow-believers. It stands to reason. I mean how many non-Buddhists would read books about Buddhism? Not many, eh? For all the apparent controversies of my project and the gob-smacking title, my publication will reach a non-Christian audience, with me rather sneakily talking about the merits of Christianity in the final pages, giving Jesus Christ what I appropriately call 'The Last Word'.

I approach Christianity in what I consider to be different and unusual angles, including relatively unheard of bible stories, and ignoring the tiresome 'repent ye now; ye must be saved' sermonising which sends non-believers hurtling headlong in the opposite direction. As for my angry remarks, I hardly need point out that Jesus Christ was not shy at pointing out in strong terms the failings of the Jewish extremists, such as the Pharisees and the Sadducees who were not particularly good commercials for God. Jesus was particularly scornful of hypocrisy, while Paul the apostle was equally keen in his letters to make the early church aware that its morality or lack of it was in danger of undermining the fledgling faith of Christianity. Meanwhile, Stephen, the first post-Christ martyr, didn't exactly mince his words in his final, fateful speech.

Finally, I do take some satisfaction in confronting people who take themselves far too seriously, and who need to be taken down a peg or two. Hence the need for satire! More than anything, I would invite the reader to tell me how he or she would react if their neighbour or loved one has a drink problem or an 'issue' with anger management. I suggest that in such circumstances we should make our friend or relative aware of their shortcoming, rather than ignore the stinky elephant in the room, and foolishly sweep the matter of concern under the carpet. If you ever want to imagine the dreadful consequences of sweeping everything under the carpet, then take a look at the hilarious Simpsons episode where, in the absence of Marge, Homer sweeps seemingly half his house under the carpet! Consequently, in my book, I have expressed my concerns and the reader is perfectly welcome to respond via an e-mail communication. My address is listed in the Introduction.

Interviewer: Similarly, how do you square the circle where you admire alleged devil-worshipper Jimmy Page, the subversive Sex Pistols and Monty Python's Flying Circus with Christianity?

Author: Again there is a myth perpetuated that 'true' believers should only listen to Christian music, read Christian literature and disassociate ourselves from anything remotely anti-Christian. This is perfectly understandable, recognising the need not to contaminate ourselves, but as a citizen of God's earth, with all its imperfections, I feel that I can 'dig' punk rock, heavy metal or subversive comedy as both art and entertainment whilst divorcing myself from the anti-Christian ethos that may underpin them.

Interviewer: You seem to be passionate about popular music. Who are your biggest influences?

Author: The first album that I ever bought was 'Complete Madness', back in the summer of 1982. So even at an early age, I was an individual of impeccable taste. As a little nipper, I was a fan of the British ska revival between 1979 and 1981 as well as a devotee of early UB40 and Bob Marley And The Wailers. At university, I started to branch out into the likes of The Beatles, The Byrds, Cream, The Doors, The Jimi Hendrix Experience, The Kinks, The Rolling Stones, The Small Faces, and The Who. My two favourite bands are probably Led Zeppelin and Pink Floyd, and no I'm not an arty-farty old middle-class hippie. I have also recently acquired a taste for classical music, believing there to be fewer greater pleasures than to be driving along to the therapeutic sounds of Handel, Rimsky-Korsakov, Schubert, and Tchaikovsky, among others. My snobbish ambition is to familiarise myself with the various concerto and symphony numbers so that I can hold my own in a conversation with an aficionado of classical music. I guess that my new interest in classical music is compelling evidence of growing old, or else I am belatedly developing a refined taste – on a par with say 'Loonee Tunes' by Bad Manners.

Interviewer: What are your favourite albums?

Author: It is hard to choose favourite albums, but here is a selection that I have a particular liking for: Led Zeppelin's first four, virtually flawless albums; The Floyd's 'The Dark Side Of The Moon'; Neil Young's 'Harvest', Donald Fagen's 'The Nightfly', Kate Bush's debut 'The Kick Inside', The KLF's 'The White Room', Primal Scream's 'Screamadelica', Prince's 'Purple Rain', Peter Gabriel's 'Shaking The Tree' compilation, and Blondie's 'Eat To The Beat'.

Interviewer: Explain your own fascination with Monty Python's Flying Circus.

Author: My introduction to Python came via their film 'Live At The Hollywood Bowl', which is a personally recommended starting-point, considering that it is pretty much a 'greatest hits' compilation. It features such nuggets as The Camp Judges, The Philosophers' Football Match, The Silly Olympics (held every 3.7 years),

Nudge Nudge, The Argument Clinic, and Mr Smoketoomuch's rant against package holidays. I then progressed on to the first two series. In particular, I am impressed with their acting ability (covering a wide spectrum of roles) as well as their clever writing, with unexpected endings and/or punch-lines. Favourites of mine include Blackmail; the newlyweds who attempt to buy a double bed in a department store with wacky consequences; but best of all is a little-known sketch where Graham Chapman attends a job-training sort of interview where John Cleese, his writing partner (very much in character) acts a bit strange. I do like the ending where three peculiar judges enter the room and award marks. It has to be seen to be appreciated. It is in series one.

Anyhow, Monty Python appeals to me because the team were always poking fun at people who take themselves too seriously, be they accountants, bankers, clergy, police, politicians, or stockbrokers. London and the Home Counties is over-populated with such types who go to work in their shirt, tie, and briefcase, probably to the Ministry of Silly Walks, and have a hugely inflated sense of self-importance. Python was spot-on at mocking certain groups and individuals who are intoxicated with their own self-worth.

Interviewer: What do you hope to achieve from this publication?

Author: World peace and everlasting happiness for all peoples of the world. Failing that I will settle for selling numerous copies because folks I have bills to pay, so give generously, one and all. However, more than this, to paraphrase that nice Don Corleone, 'I want respect'. I think that I am long overdue for critical acclaim and recognition of my comic genius. I guess that I shouldn't hold my breath. Above all else, I hope that my publication opens doors for me, so that I am invited to contribute articles and commentaries for magazines, newspapers, radio and/or television. Perhaps I will be taken seriously as a would-be satirist or comedy scriptwriter. Therefore, it is my aspiration that this book is a commercial for my talents and expertise (such as it is) and puts me in the shop window for work in the media. Please don't be shy out there and welcome me with open arms into new avenues, or am I expected to crawl back under the stone whence I came, condemned to a life of toiling in a call centre, surrounded by boozy floosies who are not fit to wash my socks.

Interviewer: Are you planning a sequel?

Author: I am not ruling out a sequel. It pretty much depends on how the Hollywood blockbuster movie, based on this book, fares at the box office. Apparently I am being played by Brad Pitt, though I am concerned that he will not do justice to my obvious sex appeal (sic). In truth, it may be some time before I inflict such torture on an unsuspecting public as the material for this publication is the accumulation of drivel that has been swimming impatiently around in my nervous system for a few years.

Interviewer: You state that you don't care much for action films. Are there any movies that you like?

Author: Although I generally abhor violent movies, my favourites are drawn precisely from that genre. I am especially keen on 'The Godfather' I and II as well as the incomparable 'Once Upon A Time In The West' and 'The French Connection', which is a refreshing departure from the formulaic good guy/bad guy cop movies where the bad guy gets caught and it all ends in kisses and smiles for the hero. 'The French Connection' is an exercise in gritty realism which reminds us terrifyingly that crime does pay.

I also like the dialogue in 'The Graduate' and in 'Midnight Cowboy', especially the kitchen scene in the former when Benjamin Braddock announces to his parents that he proposes to marry Elaine Robinson: "When did you discuss this, Ben"? "We haven't." "What makes you think she wants to marry you"? "She doesn't. In fact, she doesn't even like me." "This idea is a bit half-baked, Ben." "No, it's completely baked." Superb stuff. I also like 'The Ipcress File' and 'Sliver', the sexual thriller about voyeurism. My beef with most modern films is that they are merely a derivative of classic movies. I am also particularly horrified at how young people have become so de-sensitised to violence. I think that if someone was gunned down in the street, resulting in floods of blood, bystanders would nonchalantly remark "this reminds me of the movie we watched at the cinema last might." When young people become de-sensitised to violence, I fear the worst.

Interviewer: Where did you obtain the idea of conducting a mock interview?

Author: I borrowed the idea of a pseudo-interview from the back cover, I think it was, of Paul McCartney's debut album released in April 1970 when that nice Paul cleverly out-manoeuvred the other Beatles by announcing the break-up of the Fab Four in a question and answer format. Paul's crafty publicity stunt was all the more remarkable because it was he in particular, in collaboration with Beatles' manager Allen Klein six months earlier, who had urged George and John to remain tight-lipped about any pending Beatles break-up. Needless to say, Paul's treachery enraged his former band members. He may project himself as a thoroughly likeable chap, but it is my estimation that one has to get up very early in the morning to get the better of Macca, bless him.

Interviewer: Why are you writing under a pseudonym?

Author: Northern Ireland was born in 1921, long before I was, yet as a democracy it still is a relative toddler, in its infant stages. Both communal polar opposites are slowly growing up, but I feel that there are still members of each community who might be sore from my slightly savage remarks. Just how their anger will manifest itself, who knows? Therefore, I reserve the right to write under an alias until such time as knee-jerk reactions have run their course and the dust has settled. As a sibling once reminded me, "nobody likes to be criticised", so I am apprehensive about how certain individuals will 'respond'. I have enclosed my e-mail address to enable a dialogue to be constructed with anyone and everyone who wishes to express their right to reply.

I am especially fascinated about how comedians like Patrick Kielty, the 'Give My Head Peace' television comedy and 'The Folks On The Hill' show are obliging the people of the six counties to laugh at themselves. Until we learn to laugh at ourselves, instead of taking our beliefs so seriously to the point where we are prepared to kill and die for them, then I feel it is prudent to function under a pseudonym.

Interviewer: You are particularly scornful of loyalism in Ulster. Do you have some axe to grind?

Author: Definitely not. I have good memories of the big annual parades that I participated in, and in my orange lodge there is a great camaraderie. My brothers have touched me with acts of kindness that would put many 'born again' Christians to shame. It gives me no pleasure whatsoever in pouring vitriol on loyalism, which they hold dear. However, my disillusionment has accumulated through the march (excuse the pun) of time, and I can no longer keep quiet about my anxieties about loyalism, although I must repeat that my reservations are not based on any personal animosities.

If I can explain. I actually possess a deep fascination with the tumultuous French Revolution. One of the consequences of the 1790s and the subsequent Napoleonic era was the emergence of nationalism throughout Europe. Nationalism, wherever it exists, concerns me enormously. I find it to be a false religion in which its ardent followers have replaced God with the idols of 'the nation', 'the country', 'the sovereign', or in the case of the Nazis, the 'Volk'. This scenario applies very much to Ulster loyalists (and Irish nationalists too) who have distorted Christianity by grafting on to it a willingness to die and kill for their patriotism.

I have for example seen with my own two eyes Orange church services where the assembled brethren are going through the motions when they sing the hymns of praise to God, but when it comes to singing the obligatory National Anthem, they deliver it with such gusto as if their very lives depended on it. Their body language on such occasions, let me assure the reader, is a dead giveaway. Orangeism and other nationalisms are reminiscent of the idolaters in the Old Testament who in the apparent absence of God constructed their own golden calf to worship, and who elsewhere built an idol out of wood, foolishly paying homage to something that they had created with their own hands. Killing and dying for king and country is totally wrong. Only dying for Christ is acceptable, whilst killing for the supposed benefit of God is tantamount to accumulating vast personal wealth in the name of Marx. Speaking of which, I would venture to argue that nationalism wherever it exists is at least as dangerously anti-Christian as communism ever was. As I have stated, it gives me no personal pleasure in undermining the misguided convictions of Ulster's loyalists and nationalists too.

Interviewer: By criticising the tabloids, are you not concerned that you could potentially be creating powerful enemies?

Author: Que sera sera. I guess that my tirade against the trashy tabloids is my Pearl Harbor, where I get my retaliation in first, but foolishly under-estimating the potential consequences from the super-power that is the British red-tops, arising out of my unprovoked attack. Actually, I think that many tabloid journalists have reservations about the nature of their work, just like employees in other organisations aren't necessarily one hundred per cent supportive of the boss. Just because you are a coal-miner doesn't automatically mean that you are a friend of the mine-owner. I am sure that deep down every tabloid peddler of hate has a conscience. It's just that, like the rest of us, they have bills to pay, and so they are financially obliged to roll out the hypocrisy, hysteria, and outrage. After all, who's interested in good news stories when there are lies, scandal, and sensationalism to be consumed instead? There is something very revealing about tabloid readers. They tend to smoke, like violent movies, love boxing matches, and own vicious dogs. The words white trash are travelling from my brain onto the page right now.

Interviewer: You have a passion for cricket. What prompted your interest in this sport?

Author: I have a vague recollection of the first two Ashes test matches of 1981, which most England fans would be happy to forget anyhow, but I remember on the final day at Headingley in the third test, switching the television off when Australia were about 50 for 1, chasing the pitiful target of 130. Astonishingly, when I switched on again to watch the last rites of Brearley's bunch, the tourists were about a startling 105 for 9! I was just in time to see big Bob Willis send Ray Bright's middle stump cart-wheeling back towards the wicket-keeper, Bob Taylor. Could there be conceivably a finer introduction or commercial for cricket than a series entitled thereafter as 'Botham's Ashes', an exceedingly ironic title, considering that far from being cremated by the Aussies, the irrepressible Botham was burying the Australians. I particularly recall Australia's nemesis spank Lillee and company to all corners of the ground for a show-stopping century on a Saturday afternoon at Old Trafford whilst in partnership with that swashbuckling Kent batsman, Chris Tavare, who must have accumulated about a dozen runs during Botham's theatrics. Oh what sweet memories, in those pre-Warne, pre-Ponting, pre-humiliation days of yore.

Interviewer: How do you anticipate your book will be received?

Author: With open arms, I hope. Clearly, if people can read it with an open mind, I will settle for that. Basically, my book is the equivalent of a three or four hour monologue in which I wax semi-lyrically about a broad range of subjects. It is not unreasonable to expect anyone and everyone to disagree with various bits and pieces, but hopefully to concur with or even be impressed by other sentiments. Above all, this 'manifesto for living' is outspoken and thought-provoking. I anticipate a mixed response, conditioned by each reader's own attitudes and values. The question I pose is whether the reader could deliver a three or four hour monologue on his or her beliefs and remedies without other people choosing to disagree here and there. It is only perfectly natural. It comes with the territory, when one is expressing opinions.

Interviewer: Will you give the reader further clues as to who you are?

Author: Oh since you asked so nicely, I shall. I am between five foot and six foot seven inches in height, possibly either black or white, wearing clothes of different colours, possessing two arms, two legs, even two hands and two feet, not to mention two eyes, and remarkably one ear on one side of my head and another one perched on the other side. Before you suggest it, I am not the burglar who stole the television set that was reported to the police earlier in the book, although I do concede that I fit the matching description. To anyone who knows me even vaguely, quoting David Frost in 'Through The Keyhole', if you read through this book, "the clues are there"!

Interviewer: You seem to have a bee in your bum about celebrities. Is this correct?

Author: Up to a point, I don't deny it. Of course, there are entertainers who are not only genuinely talented, but who are selfless individuals who perform great acts of kindness which put me to shame. However, I remain a bit suspicious of the megalomaniac, attention-seekers who jump at the chance to appear in television commercials, charity appeals, magazine covers, and television interviews. Take the incomparably great cook and all-round good egg, Jamie Oliver. Not only does he currently have yet another television programme but I have to suffer his Sainsbury's 'try something new' advertisements, not to mention the added bonus of making an appeal for Comic Relief. Quite what he has to do with British comedy I am blissfully unaware. Right-on Jamie, the champion of all that is good and decent is about as hilarious as an episode of 'Last Of The Summer Wine'. I fully expect the universal Mr Oliver to soon be presenting the news, followed by the weather forecast, with live football commentaries thrown in for good measure. Poor old Gordon Ramsey can scarcely keep apace of Jamie's plans for world domination.

Perversely, the attention-seeking 'stars' tend to be the same spoiled brats who complain of privacy intrusion and hassle from fans. They only have themselves to blame. I just hope that I can repress my resentment of those greedy pigs who own a handful of cars, possess a handful of houses, containing a dozen bedrooms, and a wardrobe big enough to clothe five hundred people. If I'm not careful, I could slide into Mark Chapman mode and assassinate one of these wealthy peasants! Mind you, Jamie Oliver is quite safe. He would probably beat off my attack with a carving knife or hypnotise me with yet another wearisome recital of 'try something new today'.

Interviewer: You let off a lot of steam at various points in your book. What is the motivation for this?

Author: Yes, I do let rip here and there. If truth be told, my own self-portrait is far from flattering too, so it is not that I regard myself totally as a superhero, surrounded by lesser beings. I actually feel very positive about beautiful music, nature, the countryside, and the seaside, but paying tribute to such phenomena is less readable than getting cross about certain developments (or lack of them) in our society. I think above all else, I get upset at what I perceive to be inequality and injustice, which I think are collectively at the very epicentre of my rants. I do have a profound sense of fair play. I like to think that I practise what I preach. I feel a little like the original Protestant (and former Roman Catholic monk) Martin Luther whose criticisms led to self-assessment (which doesn't have to be taxing). One of the legacies of the Reformation was that the church of Rome was obliged to look at itself, and via the Council of Trent and the counter-reformation, the Roman Catholic church attempted to overcome its malaise. I sincerely hope that my strong words will prompt other people and organisations to consider the need for removing the decay, reforming, and cleaning up their act.

Interviewer: Without wishing to split hairs (or heads), you are possibly guilty of one or two contradictions. For example, you are critical of young people who drink alcohol, but you also do so. Is this correct?

Author: I can see where you are coming from. Actually, it is perfectly acceptable for a Christian to drink alcohol, so long as it is not to excess. I mean it is frequently cited that Jesus Christ's first recorded miracle was turning water into wine at the wedding in Cana. Christians are expected to be paragons of virtue, but we all have flaws and imperfections. It is possible that the reader can discern one or two contradictions in my book, but hey I'm still growing up and I welcome constructive criticism that makes me aware in the nicest possible way of my shortcomings. Perhaps therein lies a contradiction, because I have chosen to be quite scathing of other people's shortcomings, but urge constructive admonishment with reference to my own. Ultimately, I am a (young) man who still has a lot to learn, as indeed do you, my fellow reader.

Interviewer: Is it really true that your book is the answer to the world's problems?

Author: Alas no, but it's one heck of an attempt, don't you think?

Interviewer: I do the questions.

Interviewer: What is your vision of your judgment day?

Author: Well, many people envisage God flying into a Hitler-like fit of rage, shouting and screaming. However, I expect Jesus Christ, my very capable attorney, to have a quiet word in the ear of the Father, whereupon my Father offers me tea, coffee, or wine. He then reminds me at considerable length of the things that I said, thought, and did that I shouldn't have, and of the things that I didn't say, think, or do that I should have. After all, is it not natural for a father to admonish his son as well as giving him positive feedback? Besides, if the Creator is generous enough to allow me to join Him in His house forever, then who am I to argue with His grace?

Interviewer: You seem to be quite morbid in your book. Is this a fair comment?

Author: Quite so. I am what I consider to be very death-conscious. Let's face it: I don't know what I will do tomorrow, or next week (if I'm spared), or next month, or next year (if I'm spared). However, I do know one activity that I will definitely engage in, and that is death. Why should death be a taboo subject that we all sweep under the carpet? It's going to happen. There is an inevitability about it, so why not make preparations for this journey and after-life, in much the same way as we make plans for other more enjoyable adventures? Is it not the case that the overwhelming majority of terminally ill people are at peace with the looming prospect of death because they have been granted a realisation of their imminent mortality? There is nothing wrong with deciding how we want our funeral to be executed. Death is a part of life. It is the switching off of the ignition at the end of the journey. Also, with every passing day, we are slowly dying. Oh sorry for that cheerful thought that we are effectively terminally ill. Anyway, I am sure that you are dying to move on to another question.

Interviewer: A number of your pieces are quite gloomy. Do you feel sorry for yourself?

Author: Sometimes I do yes. Somebody has to! No, in all seriousness I look back at such pieces as 'I Will Go To My Grave' and even 'I Could Have Been A Contender' that I did a few months ago as merely evidence that I was not in good form at that time of writing. I will resist the temptation to remove them because although I feel very positive at the moment, they are poignant reminders of my fluctuating moods, which I am sure applies to most human animals. I liked the comment that John Lennon once made where he suggested that his songs, often spectacularly misinterpreted by others for their own ends, were simply a diary of how he felt at that given time. I think he speaks for most songwriters and writers in general, so my positive and negative contributions are indicative of having had a good or bad day at the office, so to speak.

Interviewer: What's the capital of Norway?

Author: Sorry?!

Interviewer: The capital of Norway. What is it? Do you know?

Author: What's this got to do with my book?

Interviewer: Nothing. I just thought you might know.

Author. Oslo, I think.

Interviewer: Is there anything else that you would like to say in your defence?

Author: Yes your honour. At the end of the day ...

Interviewer: It's midnight.

Author: Please don't interrupt. At the end of the day ... I've lost my train of thought now. Oh yes ... at the end of the day, I feel immensely proud and quite emotional about this book which I consider to be my Olympic gold, irrespective of the potential reaction it may garner. I would go so far as to say that it is the greatest thing that I have ever done, by a huge distance.

Interviewer: Which isn't saying much for the rest of your life.

Author: Hey, let's not have so much of your irreverent comments, thank you very much. Actually, I always wanted to be a recording artist, so I guess this conquest of Everest is the nearest that I will come to recording an album. If I could be permitted to waffle on for a few more seconds ... ?

Interviewer: Very well then. If you must.

Author: Oh yes sir, I must. I think that there is still a certain degree of intellectual snobbery in literary circles in so far as a writer is expected to compile a prose which revolves around a central plot or a handful of themes. However, I believe that a publication need not be the literary equivalent of a concept album. A scribe ought to have license to meander along an assortment of topics as I have attempted to do. For example, in the world of popular music, most albums are an amalgam of ballads, dance songs, love songs, and social commentaries. Therefore, why can a book not wander off in different directions too? Ultimately, I regard my tour de force as an album, but obviously without music. It is a kind of a Smiths' album, without any of their tunes. Alternatively, I am someone who rarely talks to many other people (like the Max von Sydow character in 'Hannah And Her Sisters'), and I even more rarely want to listen to many other people, so this manual is my efforts to talk to the world. If anybody wants to listen, and even respond, I would be happy to oblige. At least I have set the agenda, instead of having to suffer other people's tiresome topics of conversation. Here endeth the lesson.

Interviewer: Well, I thank you most sincerely for sharing your esteemed thoughts with us humble mortals.

Author: My pleasure.

Interviewer: Before you take your leave of me, could you kindly please autograph a copy of your book for me?

Author: You must be kidding. (*Exits, stage right*)

Interviewer: What a tosser. Yet another arrogant, big-headed, jumped-up wannabe. Typical writer. (*Exits, stage left*)

INFAMY, INFAMY, THEY'VE ALL GOT IT IN FOR ME

If you have been seriously affected by any of the issues raised in this volume, then the following course of action is strongly recommended:

Take six Aspirin tablets after breakfast, followed by six Aspirin after lunch, and then six more tablets after supper, washed down with half a bottle of vodka for ten weeks. If symptoms prevail, you should pay a visit to your local Member of Parliament's surgery, where he or she will probably break their election promise by failing to help you. In the last resort, you are very welcome, though rather unwise to send a strongly-worded letter of protest to the following address:

Complaints Department
c/o Crazy Diamond
Park bench, nearest one to the duck pond
St.James's Park
London
United Kingdom
(sort of in) Europe
(definitely in) The United States of the Western World
Northern Hemisphere
Freepost (no stamp necessary, but using one will keep the Royal Mail in business)
PO Box 96919070

Please allow up to ten weeks for a response due to large volume of letters anticipated.

ANSWERS TO 'FICTION OR NON-FICTION'

1 **False.** The prison rioted when a rumour spread that I might be incarcerated there. The judge at the Old Bailey was therefore obliged to release me.

2 **False.** Mind you, he did manage to become a Labour Prime Minister instead between 1945 and 1951.

3 **True.** or ask a silly question.

4 **False.** My socialist sympathies robbed me of a glittering career serving the 'needs' of Conservative male backbenchers.

5 **False.** In fact, the great Jimmy Greaves failed to score once in the 1966 World Cup finals. Small wonder he was omitted from the final. Also, Greaves's biggest claim to fame was his record of scoring on his debut for whatever team he played for, but even this deadly marksman never managed to score in a goal-less draw.

6 **False.**

7 **Emphatically true.**

8 **False.** There used to be a joke that you would never see a Scotsman playing tennis at Wimbledon, and judging by Andrew Murray's recent failures in SW19, it is not so much a joke as a fact.

9 **Two-thirds true.** The only falsity is that my birth did not occur during a Heartbeat episode which is all the more astonishing, considering that Heartbeat's life span (since about 1992) has lasted longer than the sixties themselves. Poor old Ken Horn must be stuck in a time warp.

10 **True.**

11 **False.** When I did telephone them, they noticed my telephone number on their caller display, and wisely declined to answer my call.

12 **True.** I was a former branch club vice-president for five years.

13 **False.** Don't be so ridiculous. If you believe that, you'll believe anything.

14 **False.**

15 **False.** Since the time of writing, great-uncle Leopold has died, so now I am 431st in line.

16 **False.** They actually urged me to jump.

17 **False.** The furious Fuhrer was outraged at Jesse Owens excelling at the Olympic Games, thus demolishing the fascist nonsense of white supremacy. Mind you, in the Olympic swimming pool, whites still rule the waves.

18 **True.** Au naturellement.

19 **False.** We were actually one of the few households that did possess a gun. My mother also owned offensive weapons in the kitchen, but she insists that they were only ever intended for food preparation.

20 **Half true.** There was indeed an own goal as Scotland were held 1–1 by the mighty Iran in the 1978 World Cup finals, but it was not scored by Salman Rushdie, whose own goal, 'The Satanic Verses' wasn't scored until 1989.

21 **False,** although I expect the great man (sic) to swear otherwise. In fact, anybody who manages to finish fourth or even just to finish at all in a 50 kilometres hurdle race deserves a medal. The Commonwealth Games is also not staged in an odd year, and Stockholm have mysteriously failed in their many applications to host the event.

22 **True.** They were not boy bands I hasten to add. I am much too beautiful for such combos. I was told in 1989 that "we will let you know" after my first audition. I am still waiting to hear how I 'performed', although I have a hunch that it was below par.

23 **True.** I contributed to a nail-biting show by losing narrowly in the crucial conundrum, after accumulating 85 points which is more than winners on other shows sometimes managed. I told you that I'm not just a pretty face.

24 **False.** He insists he only has two. I guess we will have to give him the benefit of the doubt.

25 **True.** Of course he is so supremely funny that he is entitled to much larger sums of license-payers money. I propose that we do a whip round at work and in our local pubs, so please give generously to such impoverished television presenters as Jonathan Woss, who is down to his last two houses and last three cars and last four holidays per year.

POST-MATCH INTERVIEW

Interviewer: Joe Cliche, you've been nominated as 'man of the match', and before you go for a desperately-needed shower, I wonder if you can give us your thoughts about the game.

Joe Cliche: At the end of the day...

Interviewer: It's midnight.

Joe Cliche: At the end of the day, the lads gave 110%, and at the end of the day, you can't ask for more.

Interviewer: What was the manager's instructions before the match?

Joe Cliche: At the end of the day, the gaffer told the lads that we had to get a result, which we did.

Interviewer: But you lost.

Joe Cliche: At the end of the day, it's still a result.

Interviewer: Joe, I can tell that you're keen to drink the 'man of the match' champagne, so I'll let you go. Back to Gary Likeable and Alan Handsome in the studio.

IDRACAB WHITE RUM

It's *cool*, it's *sexy*, it's *glamorous*. It's *irresistibly vile* and *horrible*.

DINING WITH PRESCOTT

Guest starring Gordon Ramsey, with Jamie Oliver dropping by too.

THE CAST

THE OLD TESTAMENT

THE NEW TESTAMENT

NEWS JUST IN

There are unconfirmed reports that Iran has seized a whale and two dolphins as hostages, after they strayed into Iranian waters. Meanwhile, the United Nations has announced that Hans Blix and two weapons inspectors are to tour the United States in search of weapons of mass destruction. Mr Blix, who was unavailable for comment, is rumoured to have suggested that he needs two hundred mathematics graduates and a very good calculator to record accurate findings. News is also coming in that David Cameron, in a desperate attempt to enhance his street credibility, is proposing to appoint Kate Moss as the new Drugs Czar. It is unclear whether Miss Moss will be engaged in the robust prosecution of the war against drug trafficking, or whether her role will be confined to testing the effectiveness of each illegal substance.